W9-AHZ-143

DISCARD

THE LAST ALGONQUIN

"A REMARKABLE TALE . . . A portrait of youth and age, pupil and teacher. The story of Joe passed on to his young friend is an astonishing account."   —*Publishers Weekly*

"BITTERSWEET AND REALISTIC . . . . the reader is led into the soul of the Indian to understand his resilient strength in the face of hopelessness."   —*Voice of Youth Advocates*

"AN OUTSTANDING ACCOMPLISHMENT. . . . This vibrant recreation of a culture is retold to us by Kazimiroff's son. The fascinating chronicle reads like fiction."

—*Journal of Reading*

"A POIGNANT TALE . . . outstanding reading . . . This moving account of the last of a tribe . . . is a remarkable study of the Red Man and his ways before and after the arrival of the White Man in this country."   —*The Fresno Bee*

"FULL OF ADVENTURE AND TRAGEDY as, like the African in more modern times, he is caught between two cultures, one dying and one alien."   —*The Charleston Post*

"A FINE ENTERTAINMENT . . . an unusually presented biography . . . how an old and dying culture meets one vibrant, brutal, and just coming alive."   —*Bestsellers*

THE
LAST ALGONQUIN

Theodore L. Kazimiroff

A LAUREL BOOK
Published by
Dell Publishing
a division of
Bantam Doubleday Dell Publishing Group, Inc.
666 Fifth Avenue
New York, New York 10103

If you purchased this book without a cover you should be aware that this book is stolen property. It was reported as "unsold and destroyed" to the publisher and neither the author nor the publisher has received any payment for this "stripped book."

Copyright © 1982, 1991 by Theodore L. Kazimiroff

All rights reserved. No part of this book may be reproduced or transmitted in any form or by any means, electronic or mechanical, including photocopying, recording, or by any information storage and retrieval system, without the written permission of the Publisher, except where permitted by law. For information address: Walker Publishing Company, Inc., New York, New York.

The trademark Laurel® is registered in the U.S. Patent and Trademark Office.

The trademark Dell® is registered in the U.S. Patent and Trademark Office.

ISBN: 0-440-20987-0

Reprinted by arrangement with Walker Publishing, Inc.

Printed in the United States of America

Published simultaneously in Canada

October 1991

10 9 8 7 6 5 4 3

OPM

My book is dedicated with love to Marietta, wife, mother and remarkable woman. She, and she alone, truly believed that The Last Algonquin *would ever become a reality. Also, and as sincerely, it is dedicated to Teddy and Michael, my sons. Their love of and happiness over the stories Grandpa used to tell them made the effort worthwhile for me.*

Theodore L. Kazimiroff

Acknowledgments

Each of these individuals gave me some special thing. Each added to this book in his own way. I thank them all as valued friends.

Dr. Ralph Solecki, Professor of Anthropology at Columbia University, knew my father during the early years and provided many important confirmations of my recollections. We corresponded and met frequently during various stages in the development of the manuscript.

Dr. William Kalaidjian provided unfailing support. It was his strength that brought "Dr. Theodore Kazimiroff Boulevard" into existence in The Bronx. Without his efforts, the City of New York might not have created this permanent memorial to my father.

Dr. William Tieck, author and present Borough Historian of The Bronx, provided memories based on his long friendship and professional association with my father.

Richard Koke, Curator at the New-York Historical Society, took time from his schedule to research his files in order to provide me with prints offering a flavor of the times I was writing about. These were most helpful in forming accurate mental images of places I could never have seen as they once were.

Robert Friedman, a man who knows books as treasured friends, gave me advice and invaluable suggestions on the manuscript. I am grateful to him for his patience and help.

Robert Kornfeld, author and playwright, was kind enough to share knowledge of the publishing industry, gained through many years of hard work.

Ruth Cavin, editor extraordinaire at Walker and Company, made the process of "pruning" my manuscript less painful than it could have been.

Ms. Terry Unkel typed the manuscript from my hand-written pages. For that alone I congratulate her. As typist, she was first reader of *The Last Algonquin*. Terry anxiously awaited each new installment, and for that she gets my sincere appreciation. When one's first potential critic reacts favorably, it bodes well.

Foreword

The best description I can think of for Ted Kazimiroff, Sr., whom I knew for at least forty-five years, is that of an over-engined dynamo. I met him first on Hunter Island in Pelham Bay Park, in New York City's Bronx, by chance the locale of this, his son's book. This was in the 1930s, well before the start of World War II. The shore islands of Pelham Bay Park were then still in existence, and I was exploring for Indian artifacts in an area that looked much as it must have to Joe Two Trees.

Later, Ted invited me to his home. I admired his artifacts, which he had surface-collected on the beaches, and was shown the amazing family garden, where were planted a whole variety of trees, causing me to wonder how in such a confined space all of them could grow and thrive.

Our paths crossed intermittently. Ted had graduated college and gone on to dental school at New York University when I met him again. This time I was in a dentist's chair at the school and Ted was supervising beginning dental students. I was then attending college myself. Much later in life, I became one of Ted's many patient patients, often eavesdropping unabashedly on the telephone calls from his construction-men "scouts" and numerous others who wanted to talk to Ted about practically everything under the sun. And he appeared to have an educated opinion about many things.

I took several trips with Ted. After a session at his dentist's chair, we would have lunch at the old mill in Bronx Park at the

New York Botanical Garden. From there we would go around
to see a little Fordham gneiss rock shelter in the woods, where
Ted had made an excavation for Indian artifacts years before.
Once we stopped on the way by the side of the Bronx River to
inspect and photograph a small boulder on which was pecked
out the life-sized likeness of a turtle. This may well have been
the mark of the Turtle Clan in the story of Joe Two Trees.

On another excursion, we went to the eastern shore of the
Harlem River below Fordham Road, where we collected non-
native flint which must have come over as ballast in the holds
of English sailing ships probably about 250 years ago. Ted,
always the instructor, filled me with the lore of the neighbor-
hood, the history of which he must have absorbed through the
very pores of his skin from many years of study and investigation.

His skills and knowledge were such that in 1965 we tried to
get funds to enable Ted to join Columbia University's dig in
Iraq, to study the dentition of some early Neolithic skeletons
we had found there, but sadly, his part of the project never
materialized.

One of Ted's numerous activities was that of official historian
of Bronx County, an unsalaried position in which he served
from 1953 until his death in 1980. He was president of the
Kingsbridge Historical Society, and the founder, in the 1960s,
of the Bronx Historical Society. In this latter capacity he saved
the Varian House, dating from the Revolutionary War, from
demolition, and he identified a sunken forest off the shores of
Pelham Bay Park that has been dated back some 3,000 years.
He was a fellow of and consultant to the New York Zoological
Society and the New York Botanical Garden, where he knew
the scientists there on a first-name basis and communicated
with them regularly.

Ted was an ecologist before the word became popular, and a
conservationist well before it became fashionable and news-
worthy to be one. He sparked the establishment of the wildlife
preserve in the Pelham Bay area, the Thomas Pell Wildlife
Sanctuary. He led memorable tours along the Bronx River in
Bronx Park, imparting his intimate knowledge of that region's
natural history to a grateful public. And perhaps the biggest
disappointment of his life was the failure of his struggle against

what he called "the monstrous rape of Pelham Bay Park"—the dumping there of what the city euphemistically called "landfill," but what is simply garbage.

As everyone who knew him can corroborate, Ted's basement and study were (and still are) filled to overflowing with more than a million artifacts, which he had hoped to find time to write about one day. Indeed, were it not for Ted Kazimiroff, archaeologists of today would not have even a fraction of the data on the New York City area that now exists because he had the skill and determination to salvage it.

Ted's profession as a dentist brought him into contact with many personalities from all walks of life and his friends are legion. But I think Ted missed his calling. With his natural talent for field research and as a teacher, he should have been on the faculty of one of our universities. He and I had long planned to write a book together on the archaeology of New York City. That was not to be. But Ted's son has created in these pages another book which in a very real sense is the senior Kazimiroff's. I am grateful that the son has so ably captured the spirit of my friend, his father.

Ralph S. Solecki
September, 1981

Contents

Introduction   xvii

Part I: The Boy and the Indian   **1**
 Chapter 1: A Strange Meeting   3
 Chapter 2: A Clay Pot   9
 Chapter 3: How "Medicine" Came to Be   19
 Chapter 4: A Gift Is Passed Across the Ages   22
 Chapter 5: "Indian Fishing"   30

Part II: Joe Two Trees   **37**
 Chapter 6: The Joining of Two Clans   39
 Chapter 7: Last of the Turtle Clan   45
 Chapter 8: The American City—New York   49
 Chapter 9: A Wounded Fugitive   57
 Chapter 10: The Hardest Winter   63
 Chapter 11: The Cave Bear   80
 Chapter 12: The Coal Mine   87
 Chapter 13: Indian Again   99
 Chapter 14: The Red-Haired Woman   105
 Chapter 15: The Ycllow-Eyed Dog   132
 Chapter 16: A Dugout Canoe   141
 Chapter 17: On the Hudson River   148
 Chapter 18: The Attack   155
 Chapter 19: Monatun   166
 Chapter 20: To the Land of His Ancestors   181

Afterthoughts   189

Index   191

The spelling of the word "Algonquin" used throughout this book was chosen because it is the most familiar to the general reader. The name has many spellings, since all are transcriptions of a spoken word: "Algonkin," "Algonkan," "Algonquian" and "Algonkian." Various versions have prevailed for a period and then died away. My own personal choice would have been "Algonkian," which is my interpretation of the word as it was spoken to my father, and many years later, to me. However, it was felt that this form might puzzle many readers, and so we have elected to use the one that is the most readily recognizable today.

Introduction

Here, at the outset, I think it is necessary to provide a definition for the story you are about to read. It is a "hand-me-down."

Unlike most of these, however, it is separated from its initial source by more than a year or two. Several generations have had a hand in the molding of this effort.

I must point out that many facts and incidents were certainly lost or distorted during the passage of the years. My own lapses are almost surely no less than those of my father, of Joe Two Trees himself, or of his own parents for that matter. I have tried to strike a good balance between the facts I know to be accurate, and the need to "flesh out" the story with material from my own experiences.

Ever since my father originally told me the basic events in the life of Joe Two Trees, I have always felt this story was too valuable to lose. I have tried to present all the salient points, as well and as truly as I could, to keep Joe's story alive.

Does this mean the book can be read as a historical document, an accurate biography? Probably not. Is it a work of fiction born of my mind? Definitely not! My late father and his native American mentor would not have stood for any such thing, and my wish is to be as faithful as I can to the story as I received it from them.

I can only hope that my efforts may someday be weighed by them, in a happier hunting ground, and found not wanting.

I hope you, the reader, will also be pleased.

Once, not very long ago, a hardy race of people spread across this continent. They extended from the Arctic to the tropics and from sea to sea. This people, for their basic stock was one, achieved high levels of culture and civilization in some parts of North America. In other parts they subsisted as wandering nomads, hunting and gathering as they followed the seasons.

Scientific evidence tells us they came from the West, across a bridge of dry land that once rose from the Bering Sea to join Asia and Alaska. They migrated in search of better hunting grounds, better homes, and probably out of curiosity to know the unknown. They traveled, over many thousands of years, braving glaciers and wild, predatory animals, to the shores of the Atlantic Ocean. Here, with no place left to go, these early Indians established their homes along the coast. As time passed, they separated themselves into nations and tribes. Those who eventually became the Algonquins of what is now New York City are the ones from whom this story stems.

While these Indians were living in this woodland paradise, another race looked across the broad Atlantic from the East. The two races had never met, and were separated by more than an ocean alone; they were also separated by something we call technology. The Europeans knew how to use gunpowder and iron, and could accomplish things the Indians had never achieved. To such a race, the conquest of a mighty ocean, in search of new lands, was fated.

Inevitably, when the two alien cultures met, the strong soon overpowered the weak, and the tenants of many thousand years were dispossessed by the new landlords. Guns and iron weapons proved strategically superior to stone and bone, and in a frighteningly short time, the once proud Indian nations were decimated by a horde of land-hungry immigrants from across the sea.

By the time these immigrants finally formed a nation for themselves, and put their former homes forever behind them, they had little left here in the form of an "Indian problem." They eliminated that small remnant by killing most survivors outright. Those pockets of Indian survivors that still remained, here and there, across the new nation were herded into areas designated as "reservations," although they have been called harsher names.

That was the situation for many years. Sometimes it was better, but usually worse. Those Indians were never brought into the larger community by any more than token actions of the white man's government. They were deprived of their homelands and way of life, and of their very culture. And then, in 1924, the U.S. government, with a twinge of conscience, ordered that these first Americans be granted American citizenship. Some may have been grateful, others were not, but most didn't even care.

By that time, the issue, here in New York, was academic. Buildings had been built, and commerce was flourishing, the population grew daily, people strolled in wooded parks, but no one had seen a real Indian for a long, long time. In any practical sense, the race, as it had been, was extinct here.

The word "extinct" has such a terrible sound. The dinosaurs are extinct, as are the woolly mammoths, and very nearly even the American eagle. The list could go on to such length that it would begin to seem impossible anything is still left. When I was a small boy, I sometimes countered that concept of extinction in a way that only children can. I would often go to the wooded places, armed with the bright eyes of youth, to search earnestly for a baby dinosaur. I was sure, with young trust, that my belief would bring one to me. Somehow, I never managed to find my small anachronism, but perhaps I grew up too soon. Take heart, though, he's still waiting out there, among the trees and hills, for my children, or yours.

Do you doubt that? I can tell you of a man who accidentally found something seemingly just as extinct, and of how the discovery shaped and changed his life. The man was my father, Dr. Theodore Kazimiroff. This book is not solely about him, however, but rather it is an attempt to chronicle the life and adventures of another man, and tell how their two lives were intertwined for several months in 1924.

The roots of this story lie, long buried, in the prehistoric Indian villages now covered by streets and apartment houses in New York City's Borough of The Bronx. The lost Algonquin people of Keskeskek and Wanaqua, which is now The Bronx, were the seed from which this story grew. The last of these people lived into my father's time.

His name, Joe Two Trees, was a combination of the two cultures. You will understand that name later on.

In 1924, on a day that can only be called fateful, my father met Joe Two Trees in what is now Pelham Bay Park in the northeast Bronx. They became friends, this oddly matched pair, and the man told his story to the young white boy. He also did something more. By his telling and teaching, he instilled in the boy a vibrant interest in the history and lore of their common homeland. The boy had Joe's companionship for only a short while, but it was long enough. His life was affected in such a fashion that the outdoors became his heaven, the preservation of mementoes from the past his sacred duty.

The boy went on to become a dentist, and for the rest of his life that was his profession. But his avocation was a far different thing. He became as well a noted archeologist, naturalist, lecturer, writer and finally, official historian of the Borough of The Bronx. His true calling was found as self-appointed preserver of our past. During the years until 1980, when he died, he excavated, collected and catalogued a museum full of artifacts, books, maps, and documents that can only partially be described by the word "vast." The Indian portion of the collection alone comprises over 200,000 articles. In addition, there are innumerable colonial and Revolutionary War artifacts. The entire collection is well over a million pieces.

Many of my father's patients can still recall being virtually left with mouth wide open as, after a phone call, the doctor jumped into coveralls and rubber boots and left. He must have had half the building and highway construction crews in New York City scouting for him. Whenever they dug into anything historically interesting, such as shells, charcoal, bones or old foundations, they'd call Dr. Kazimiroff.

It is quite possible that during his life he dug up more of the city than Consolidated Edison. He accumulated a tremendous number of specimens with historical significance, and preserved them as a means of adding to the store of our knowledge of the past. His accomplishments in the fields of landmark preservation and ecology are endless.

I have often been asked what drove him to such lengths, and I've given that question a good deal of thought. The only real answer that has ever come to me is that all the digging didn't really start with a shovel at all. It started with an encounter. I think he was worried that a very old Algonquin gentleman might otherwise be forever forgotten.

I remember that it was a weekend morning in June of 1950. My father had been doing some work on a small Indian village site which he'd discovered in Riverdale, in the northwest corner of the Bronx alongside the Hudson River. That morning, he asked if I'd like to come along and see the area where he was digging and making his measurements. Naturally, we were off and gone in no time flat.

During most of the morning, we measured and recorded the spots where pottery shards, bone fragments from food remains, and other items were found. Later, as we were digging an exploratory trench, we cut into reddish earth, and then darkened stones and soil. Soon, we had decided it was a probable fire pit, the central point of an old Indian hut. In order to verify this, we started working slowly away from the blackened area, clearing a circular pattern. We were looking, my father said, for evidence of post holes. These remains of the upright members for the dwelling would prove we had found the site of an actual family cooking and heating fire, and not just some camping spot used by a wandering hunter.

I was surprised that we would be able to find wooden posts not rotted after hundreds or thousands of years in the soil, and I asked my father about that. His explanation was probably the most important thing that I ever learned about searching for the past. From it derives much of my personal philosophy of archeology.

"Ted," he said, "the ground under our feet is very much like a time capsule. When men want to save something and send it on to future generations they take great pains to put it in a container that will preserve it and not allow the contents to change down through the years. Then, some day, men who were not even born when the capsule was made open it, and if they have sufficient wisdom, they cherish the contents; use them to learn their heritage and know their ancestors.

"The time capsule under our feet isn't perfect, but every mark that is on the earth, every item that is buried in it, leaves some trace. This may last for months, years, centuries, and even longer. We don't open our capsule with a key as such, we use a shovel, a pointing trowel, a penknife blade, or even a toothpick.

"When the wooden posts deteriorated and the wood was absorbed into the soil, a very specific chain of events took place. The soil, which had been compressed when the posts were driven, would have stayed forced aside and the holes gradually left with only the darkened remains of wood. Silt eventually filtered into the crevices and filled the area up again. So, we must look for a pattern of darkened, round marks surrounding our fire pit. If the soil has never been disturbed, and if we are very lucky, we'll find that evidence today."

Well, we were lucky, and just before it got dark, we had cleared and cleaned enough ground to see a distinct pattern in the soil. The post holes were there, and we both knew we had hit the digger's jackpot.

The fire pit of an Indian dwelling can be one of the best of all possible spots to hunt for artifacts. Broken pottery or tools often found their way into the pit, along with meal remnants and even, on occasion, human remains.

Why would Indian human bones be found in the family fire pit? Have you ever taken a shovel and tried, in January or February, to dig a hole of any consequence in the frozen ground? With modern implements of steel, the job is very difficult. With primitive tools of wood and stone, the same job becomes impossible.

Put yourself in place of an Indian family with a winter death. You must bury your lost one in the only soft ground available, and that is the family fire pit. The fire which burns every day keeps that spot soft. A grave is scraped out and lined with evergreen boughs so that the dead one will not be touching the cold, bare earth. He is bent into a fetal position and placed in the former fire area. Being a frugal family, of a frugal tribe, you bury just a few necessary items with the departing member so he can make his camps, and hunt during his journey to the hereafter, or Happy Hunting Ground. You know that he must make campfires each night because always, you have looked into the evening skies and seen the band of white glow that reaches away from the Earth and into the heavens. The people have said that this is the campfires of the dead on their way to paradise.

After a suitable time has passed, you stop mourning, for now he has passed over the Milky Way and hunts in fields of game where winter never comes. He fishes in streams full of trout and, at last, is with the Great Spirit, Tchi-Manitou.

When the time is right, the family gathers outside the wigwam on a clear night, and chooses a star to become the visible embodiment of the spirit lost. Although he is now a part of the firmament, he is not quite gone. Sometimes, when the creatures of the night cry, or wind sighs in the pines, the voice of the departed is to be heard. One can never be completely sure that the wolf is really a wolf, or that the bear is not trying to talk to you.

Long ago an Iroquois war party from the North took a young Algonquin boy. His family, somehow, managed to recover his body. His was the skeleton which I helped my father unearth during many trips in that June of 1950. He never reached the Iroquois lands to the North, to become a slave. Was he killed because he resisted and attempted to escape?

His family performed the rituals and they buried him in the fire pit. They moved the dwelling to another spot. When they buried him, his body held three triangular arrow tips, of the type that were meant never to be withdrawn from the victim. His legs had both been broken above and below each knee. He had four broken ribs, both hands had been crushed and his skull was smashed in.

We wondered many times, over the years, what he might have done to cause his captors to treat him in such savage fashion. The time capsule had given us a grisly tale, a story made up of parts. Some we have; some we never can. We can't detail the heroic efforts that must have been required for his family to reclaim their dead son. We did, however, find a pattern as we excavated sites and classified them chronologically. We found that more and more Iroquois influence came into the Algonquin culture as the years passed on toward the arrival of the white man. Our time capsule showed us a tribe in serious trouble, preyed upon by a stronger, more warlike people. The makers of triangular arrowheads seemed bent upon dominating or destroying the more peaceful Algonquins.

Among the Indian bands that traded and took items for tribute from lesser tribes, a high esteem was universally placed upon Sewan, also called wampum. This material, made from beads of shell, was prized by the Iroquois who had no easy access to the raw materials. The problem was solved by making the Algonquins pay annual tribute in wampum and other valued commodities.

Far inland, in what was once Iroquois territory, excavations generally uncover hundreds of these beads. In New York City and Long Island, where the wampum was made, very few beads have been discovered.

One can easily see the Algonquin predicament. Pressed to find food enough for their own use, unable to spend sufficient time to prepare for their needs, they must now further weaken their tribe by paying tribute to the ones who called themselves "wolf people."

But even deadlier enemies were climbing into ships that would soon bring them here to build a nation. By the time the Liberty Bell was tolling the intentions of these new colonists, the Indians along the northern Atlantic coast could already find no place left to call their own. Broken and weakened, they retreated further and further from the white invasion, until a last few were all that remained of a mighty, ancient culture. The beaver left, the last bear was killed, the deer died, and the last Algonquins were gone from Manhattan Island. By the end of the 18th century, they had moved toward the north, perhaps to New York's Westchester County or Connecticut, via the Bronx, to escape these people who could kill with a noise from a long stick.

It was against a backdrop of information such as this that I grew up. It was only natural that such sagas would fire my imagination and make me clamor to be included in the digging. My requests didn't fall on deaf ears, and during the years of my childhood I helped my father in his work of seeking out Indian sites and relics with increasing frequency. We dug so much earth out of so many places that I often thought we should have been miners. In retrospect, I suppose we were miners of a sort. The act of mining is generally thought of as removing some precious resource from the covering earth or stone. This was certainly our goal. Each pottery shard, each arrowhead, stone tool, and especially each burial pit, gave us a little better insight into the New York of long ago. It was our goal to save these relics from loss or destruction.

We explored all the sites of native habitation that have become classics in the existing literature. But we also found unknown prehistoric villages and campsites on our own. Soon, we were specializing in undisturbed habitations. The apparent ease with which we found them puzzled me.

It was in this way that we "discovered" ancient camping sites and villages in Riverdale, along the Bronx River in the New York Botanical Gardens, at many spots along the shore of Long Island Sound and even on some of its larger islands such as Hart, High, and Glen. But gradually our area of specialization narrowed down to Hunter Island and Pelham Bay Park. There my father's guesses were infallible, and many finely made stone tools and implements joined our collection. We uncovered earthenware cooking pots, bone fishing utensils and even the obvious weapons of Indian warfare. Often, we also uncovered the victims of those early Indian wars. For thousands of years, and even into the era of early white settlers, vicious battles had been fought in our digging area.

Sometimes I had the distinct idea that my father knew, before we found it, exactly what we were looking for. Something seemed to direct him to a particular large oak tree, or glacial boulder. He would then look in a given direction, pace off what seemed a predetermined number of steps and put down his knapsack and gear. There we would dig, usually with success.

This seeming magic was simply too much for a young boy to overlook, and although he carried it out with an air of humor, my father never gave me any real explanation of his uncanny foreknowledge until one day during the summer of 1952. I can still clearly remember sitting upon a big rock and listening, fascinated, as my father started to tell me the story of Joe Two Trees, last known member of the Weckquaesgek tribe of the Algonquin Nation, a man my father had met in the then wilderness of Pelham Bay Park when he was a young boy.

I

The Boy
and the Indian

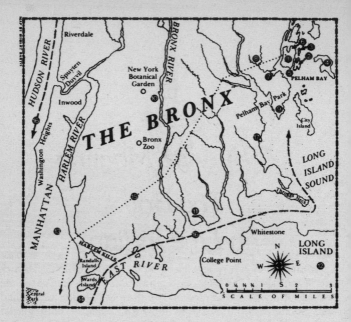

This map shows The Bronx as it was when the Indians left. Very few "improvements" had been made yet. The great land-moving projects and landfill ventures of the 1930s and 1940s hadn't happened. Hunter Island was still an island. The Bronx was not incorporated as a county of New York City until 1914.

1 Hunter Island
2 Twin Island
3 Two Trees Island
4 Hart Island
5 Mishow
6 Saxon Stone
7 Vagabond Bay
8 Site of Pell land purchase in 1654
9 Revolutionary War landing by British General Sir William Howe
10 Aquehonga, sold to Jonas Bronck in 1641
11 Snak-a-pins
12 Sewan-Hacky (Long Island)
13 Manhattan Island
14 Hell Gate (Monatun)
15 Joe Two Trees's probable route from Hunter Island to New York City
16 Joe's river route back to Hunter Island
17 Dr. Theodore Kazimiroff's boyhood home

1

A Strange Meeting

When I was a boy in 1924, began my father, I used to walk from my house in Throggs Neck to the woody hills of Hunter and Twin Islands as often as I could. That area fascinated me because it contained almost all the flora and fauna that I had read about in my Boy Scout manuals. I found both glacial boulders and scratches, evidence of the great ice sheet that had descended on the Bronx from the North. I picked and ate berries and fruits of varieties my mother never saw in stores. The rocky shores provided me with ample specimens for my geology studies. Fresh water ran from several springs on the islands, and so I could be self-sufficient for a day, without even bringing along a lunch or canteen. There was no Orchard Beach here yet to attract people in any number, and often I could spend an entire day walking field and shore without seeing another person. I had no idea then that the reverse was seldom true. When a bush would quiver without a breeze to prod it, I would dismiss it as a small animal frightened by my intrusion into this solitude. For many months I was quite unaware that I was being watched.

Then one day I discovered a rabbit run in the underbrush. It was heavily tamped down, indicating the passage of many little feet. I decided to follow it and see if I could stalk up to a cottontail and touch him. I had touched a deer that way once at the Boy Scout camp upstate.

For a while it was easy going as I followed through the low

brush, but as I went along it became heavier. Soon I was on all
fours, crawling under blackberry brambles and thick bushes. A
few feet ahead, a cut branch caught my eye and I went over to
take a closer look. The cut wood was all that showed of a very
ingenious noose-snare, made entirely of wood and bark strips.
During the following months, alerted by the snare I had found,
I quietly noticed other signs of possible habitation in my woodland retreat. The possibility that someone could live here,
unobserved by even so regular a visitor as myself, was intrigu-
ing. I continued my observation through the summer and into
the early fall. I was studying the animal life and the botanical
and geological portions in preparation for several merit badges
I wanted for my scouting efforts. And I always looked, as well,
for the person I now knew to be there, but I could never find
him.

One morning in early October of that year, I was on Twin
Island. As I walked toward the glacial boulder called "Lion
Rock" a figure stepped from behind it into my view. He stood
and looked at me for what seemed quite a long time before he
said, "Good day, I am Joe." I remember thinking, even after
those few words, that he had a foreign accent of a sort I had
never heard. How mistaken I was! That accent was only foreign
to my ears. It was anything else but that to this land of oak
trees and blackberries. I didn't know it yet, but I was speaking
to a true American, an Algonquin Indian!

The second thing that Joe said was, "I know you very much.
You watch all the living things, but you do not harm them.
Why?" I tried to explain to him about my interest in natural
history and my scouting merit badges, but I think he didn't
understand all of it. At some point in our conversation, he
decided that scouting was like "being Indian." When that concept had formed in his mind he seemed more at ease with me.
Finally, he told me he hoped I would have my merit badges,
and he left me to lean on the Lion Rock and wonder. As he
walked away I noticed several things about him. His long gray
hair and wrinkled face plainly showed great age, but his posture was straight, almost military, with shoulders held stiffly.
He was quite tall, perhaps six feet, and lean to the point of

boniness. Over his gaunt frame hung a patchwork of clothes made from fur, cloth, and leather.

After that day Joe no longer hid from me, and he would often accompany me on my forays. His knowledge of the woods around us was phenomenal, but he was often confused by my words. If I asked him to show me the heron, he would shrug as if to say "such words are not mine." But if I asked him for the fishing bird with the long neck and pointed beak, he would smile and off we'd go.

In the terms of a modern naturalist, he knew hardly any of the creatures' names. In terms of their lives and hidden places, he knew them all as neighbors. They were his actual, lifelong neighbors, for he had lived here all of his days except for a few years during which he tried unsuccessfully to adapt to the life of New York City and other white man's places.

Joe never actually told me he was an Indian. He seemed to think I should know it automatically, gradually, and that is exactly what happened. I knew. The realization crept up on me over a period of months and finally it was there. I was aware that Joe was an Indian, and somehow, the knowledge did not seem surprising. We had become friends during that winter and when he saw that I had guessed his origins and was still not a threat, he asked if I would hear his story so that it would not die when he went to the Great Spirit. Since all his people were gone now, he knew that when his bones were in the ground no one would be left to speak of him or of his deeds during the storytelling time of future winters. He warned me sternly that Tchi-Manitou, maker of all things, is very strict about the telling of stories. If I ever told the story after he was gone, said Joe, it must only be in the winter, otherwise, the Maker would become angry with me for interrupting the time when His people should fish and plant and put aside food for the long winter. The cold season was the correct time for telling stories.

He took a long time to explain to me the importance of his story. He told me that by itself it was only the history of his life, which had not been as great with war deeds and valor as past braves. The importance, he said, was in the fact that only when no one knew his story, only when no one was left to tell it at the campfire of winter, would he be truly gone. As long as one person could still tell the tale, Two Trees, for that was his

Algonquin name, would still live in the rocks and trees that had been his home.

He asked if I would visit his home, and naturally I agreed. We set off at a brisk walk across Hunter Island to a spot near one of the clear springs that had given me water on many a summer day. Joe said, "Here we are." I looked, but saw nothing to indicate a house or any sort of habitation. Joe walked to a very thick, brushy wall that consisted of poison ivy, thorn bushes, and ropy vines of Virginia creeper, and seemed to melt right through the tangled barrier. Although I hadn't been able to see it, there was an entranceway.

Once I had passed through, I looked around and saw that the foliage formed a roughly circular barrier wall about fifty or sixty feet in diameter. One side of the clearing had been cultivated into neat piles of earth, and a gigantic cornstalk grew from each pile. Between the corn, at ground level, creepers spread in all directions. At intervals along these vines, large squash peeked out of the broad leaves.

The other half of the tiny circle held dozens of small poles, and beans were evident in the many green pods that hung down from the covering vines. Tomato plants also had a small patch devoted to their yellow flowers and greenish fruits.

Directly across from the hidden entrance stood a low bark hut or shelter. Its frame was made of bent saplings and its covering was a combination of woven reeds, mud, and slabs of elm bark. It looked long enough for a man to lie at full length in, but barely. Along one wall of the structure many fruits and vegetables were cut open and spread out to dry in the sun.

The size of the plants and their fruits was such that I asked Joe how he got them to grow so large. My father grew many of these in our home garden patch, with fertilizers and insect powders, but his were never so perfect. Joe told me the heads and entrails of all fish that he caught were used to enrich the soil of his small plot. Plenty of water from the nearby spring was carted up to keep the soil moist, and the Maker's sun did the rest.

Joe explained how he kept his small farm free of pests. The Indian form of insect control was fascinating, and maybe modern farmers would do well to use a bit less poison and a few more of these earlier tricks.

Joe said that each fall, when the leaves had dropped, he would walk among the blackberry and alder patches. Here he found the egg cases of the praying mantis. He would collect as many as he could find and place them at intervals around his compound. In spring, when his crops were beginning to grow, hordes of hungry mantises would hatch out to eat the young beetles bent on devouring leaves and vegetables. A side benefit for Joe was that the growing predators would eat flies and mosquitos all summer long as well.

Joe had found that the orange and black beetle we call lady bug was not very appetizing to the praying mantis. They, however, were fond of eating the tiny aphids that sucked the juices from the tomato plants. When he found a lady bug in his travels he would carefully place it in his belt pouch and bring it home. The tiny bug was then placed on a tomato plant to eat heartily of the little aphids.

Here was a man who had created an ecological balance in his surroundings long before ecology became a fashionable word. The maximum use of all things, within a framework of no waste, was something Joe did as his ancestors had for thousands of years. He lived this way, apparently, for no other reason than that it made good sense.

As I looked around the small homesite, I was struck by the strange mixture of twentieth-century and Stone-Age artifacts that stood here and there, ready for use. A rusted and broken shovel leaned against a low rock and beside it was a stone hoe lashed to a hickory handle with strips of bark. On the overhanging branch of a tree hung a long pole with a carefully carved bone head. The tip had many barbs, and was evidently a fish spear. Near some empty tin cans (probably scavenged from the shoreline) and a battered cast iron pot stood a cooking vessel made of clay. It looked just like the ones I had seen in the Indian exhibit at the American Museum of Natural History in New York City. I told this to Joe.

I guess he saw the interest that the clay pot had aroused in me, and his next question came as something of a surprise. "You want to make one? I help you." So it was that the first Indian project in what was to become a long list was undertaken by a young white boy, long after the original race was gone—almost.

I had already learned that Joe held magical meanings and spiritual concepts very important, but his explanation of the making of a simple pot was astounding. He told me that this making must begin first in the heart, or soul, for that was the place the Maker started all good ideas. Once the young thought had ripened, like a fruit on its branch, it would follow a natural course to the head. The brain, he said, was the second stopping place for any plan. It was in the brain that Tchi-Manitou would come during sleep time to help the plan become a workable project. In short, once the new idea had been prayed over, thought about, and then slept on, it was time to bring it into the world, as a reality. I was told to go home and pray that my pot would be made well, and that once made, it would be full whenever I, or my family, was hungry. Joe Two Trees wasn't very particular about who I prayed to, since he seemed quite certain that my prayers would find their way to the appropriate authority even if I called Him by some name he didn't know.

I undertook the making of my pot as I had been instructed, and the old man's sincerity made me feel it was really the only course of action I could take. Anyway, I thought, a prayer for a full, family cooking pot could hardly be a wasted one.

2

A Clay Pot

The next day I walked to Hunter Island and, as usual, Joe found me before I found him. We passed the early hours of the morning drinking a tea that he had made from the berries of the sumac plant. Each fall he would gather the berries when they turned as red as the sundown. For the rest of the season he boiled these with the broad leaves of green seaweed to make a healthful drink. It was this beverage, he claimed, that prevented colds, arthritis, coughs, and other illnesses. It didn't taste awfully good.

After passing the early part of the warm, sunny morning at these amenities, I told Joe I was ready to start the making of my pot. He seemed quite surprised and asked if the Great Spirit had already sent instructions to my hands about the making of a thing so important as a vessel to use in the cooking of His game. He asked me if the Maker himself had told me to start on the path that would end with a new clay pot. I was still a small bit dubious, but I answered that He had. Two Trees told me that to start the pot before the sanction of Tchi-Manitou would be very bad medicine.

Since my interpretation of "medicine" was the bad-tasting stuff that comes out of brown bottles when I got a fever, I asked him to explain. He gave his concept to me, and I have preferred it to mine ever since. "At the beginning, when the Great Spirit was just finishing the making of all things, He saw that He still had some power left over. This was power that He had not needed to use in making the water and land, or the mountains and trees, or any of the living things. In order that this power should not be let loose to be lost, or fall into the hands of Manetto, the evil one, He saw that He must find some use for it. He sat down for a time to think, and smoked his pipe. Seeing the clouds that He made, He thought that they would be good to make shade for His new creations and He told them to continue in the skies forever. So that they could do this, He gave each of them some of the leftover power.

"Having made the clouds, and given them some of His power, He decided to share the rest among all the other creations of the world in proportion to their rank in the overall order of things. He shared it with the rocks and animals, trees, birds, humans, and all other things. It was in this way that all things came to have power or medicine. If we can be very skillful, or lucky, when we make something from any of these, we may use materials that are more full of good medicine than others. In this way we can end up with a finished product that will be very full of medicine for its intended use."

Since my clay pot would be an important item, it was necessary that we use materials that had good medicine in them. He told me to go to the beach and find ten large, clean oyster shells, indicating the number with the fingers of his two hands. When I came back with these, he examined them critically one by one. Apparently they were satisfactory. Then he told me to clean them further with sand and fresh spring water. I did this. We then placed them on a large rock to dry in the sun.

Joe said that while the shells were drying I could begin to collect the clay that would be used. At a spring on the other side of Hunter Island, above the high-tide line, we began to dig out handfuls of bluish-gray clay. This was the only clay, he said, that would dry correctly and not crack in the fire afterwards.

We carried the clay back to Joe's camp on two slabs of elm tree bark. When we were back inside the campground, we sat down on the ground and squeezed the clay through our fingers until no pebbles or lumps remained. It was now of a very uniform consistency, but a bit on the wet side.

Then the man explained the use of the oyster shells. While the clay stood to dry a bit, I took the shells to a flat stone and ground them up into a fine, white powder. The rounded, flat mulling stone that Joe used to grind up his corn served very well, and soon I had a fairly large pile of shell dust.

Joe examined the pile, and without a word, divided it in two. Half the pile he took and scattered around his vegetable plot. The other half he poured into my clay mixture.

I sat and squeezed the powder into the clay, mixing the two into one. All the while I wondered about the part that had gone into the garden soil. Joe never spoke of it again, and I never asked. It was only years later that I decided I had ground some calcium to keep the soil "sweet," or nonacid. Five shells would have been sufficient for my pot, but five would not have done a thing for Joe's tomatoes. At the time, I had considered ten shells an invaluable step in the mystical making of a clay pot. Somehow, I'll never be sure that it wasn't.

Everything had been done properly, he assured. The shell dust would give its medicine to the clay, making it stronger than it would have been alone. The mixture was clear of any foreign material such as pebbles or twigs, and now it was ready to form into a pot.

First, under the watchful eyes of my Indian mentor, I modeled a small, round, bowl-shaped base. I set this aside to dry and stiffen a bit while I kneaded and rolled small ropes of clay. I placed these, one next to another, on a smooth sheet of bark. Joe made sure that they were the proper thickness and length. Any that didn't measure up to his standards went back into the general mix to be rolled out again.

He explained that each must be slightly longer and thinner than the previous one. This was what would make the pot grow from its thick-walled, narrow base to its thinner but wider rim.

I went back to my base piece then and found that it had set sufficiently to serve as a foundation for my first coil of clay rope. I laid the roll around the periphery of the base piece, and carefully pinched the two ends together. With the dabbing on of a bit of wetter clay, the joint was soon invisible. We added two or three more coils in the same way, and then he said we would wait and let this part set so the pot-to-be would not slump and cave in from its own weight.

After an hour in the warm, dry air, the first portion of my vessel had dried sufficiently to take the weight of more clay coils. I added the next group, trying not to let my excitement take away from the careful work that the man kept reminding me to do. That wasn't easy, for I could now see the beginnings of a recognizable form. It wasn't a pot yet by any means, but it was far from a mixture of clay and oyster shell dust.

I repeated the routine at intervals during the remaining daylight. By the time shadows were long and the whippoorwills had started their mournful song, I saw that the pot would not be finished that day. We covered the still-damp form with wet leaves to keep it from drying too fast. If that should occur, he told me, further coils would not stick well, and the whole pot would crack when we placed it in fire to harden.

I went home and told my parents about the pot at supper that night. I remember that my mother didn't seem too impressed. She said she could remember stories of people making such pots of clay in her native Russia, but that it didn't seem to be necessary in this new country where everyone could buy a metal pot at any good houseware shop.

My father was a bit more receptive since he, as I, was very interested in the past of his new homeland. It was he, I suppose, who had first started me off on my natural history investigations. He didn't want me to become overly preoccupied with impractical matters, however, and his next statement showed it. He told me it was good that I had interesting ways to spend my vacations, but to keep in mind I would soon be big enough to spend them with him, learning the iron worker's trade. I thought this would be fine later on, but all I could think of now was the unfinished clay, under leaves at Hunter Island. The night seemed to pass more slowly than most.

Next day I greeted sunrise with Joe. We both held cups of the therapeutic tea and watched a new day wink over the eastern horizon. Now, said the Indian, that the Maker had given us the light to see by, we could resume our work.

We uncovered the damp clay, and placed it on the work surface of smooth stone. I was caught by the idea that it was beginning to look very much like an egg with the blunt end cut off. It was not a smooth egg though. Each new coil of clay had produced a ridge and now I looked at a corrugated, egg-shaped item. Joe said not to worry. Once I placed the final few coils in their positions he would show me how to smooth the pot.

I added the last clay pieces, and the pot now stood about 18 inches high. It was roughly 12 inches across at the top and tapered to a roundish point at the bottom.

Now we took the remaining clay and mixed in more spring water, bringing it to a pasty consistency. Using the palms of both hands, I smoothed this into the corrugations on the sides of my pot. Soon, all were filled, and by gently stroking the excess away, I obtained an uninterrupted curvature from base to lip.

The old man said now was the time to add the decorative marks that would make the pot pleasing to the eye. Other, "medicine," marks would need to be etched in after the pot had begun to harden. The decorations were only for people's eyes, but the later marks would be for the spirits. If they found these marks pleasing, the pot would serve its owner well.

We took a flat piece of wood and wound bark cord around it until the wood was covered with a tight wrapping. We pressed this into the still damp clay, producing a pattern of wavy lines that was intricate and yet uncomplicated. The idea was simplicity itself, but the result, as Joe had predicted, was pleasing to the eye.

Now, he said, we must be very careful to dry the pot properly. It must dry from the inside out for its first stage. We placed damp grass around the outside and left the inside empty, then left it that way for a long time.

When, later, he tested it with his finger for the third or fourth time, Joe said we could now carve in the magical marks his parents had taught him. In later years my study of archeology showed me that Joe's parents had not been the first of his ancestors to use these medicine markings on their pottery. In technical terms the etching that I did that day, with a small, pointed chip of flint, is called "Bowman's Brook"-type incising. Its use is dated as being about one to two thousand years old by today's archeologists.

Next we filled the pot with damp leaves and grass. It stayed filled overnight. This allowed the moisture to be forced out through the now drying clay.

In the morning we took away all the grass and leaves and left the pot to sun dry. Then we left it again overnight. The next day, after the morning dew had been burnt away by sun, Joe

pronounced the time for building the fire. This done, with small
chunks of dry oakwood, we let it burn down to embers. The pot
was placed among these, and we watched as the last moisture
was driven off in a fine mist of water vapor. We added new
charcoal during the day, but only enough to replace that which
was reduced to whitish ash.

Late afternoon had come when we let the final embers die
and cool off. It was important that the pot cool slowly so it
would not crack now and ruin all our efforts. The new vessel
didn't crack, and just at sundown, Joe said it was ready.

We carefully lifted the pot from its bed of ashes. It was still
quite hot to the touch, but Joe said this was good, for we still
had one step to perform. Now we must make it waterproof. If
we did not perform this last process it would never be any good
for cooking use. The water and heat would soften the clay and
make it porous.

While the original fire had been cooling, Joe built a small bed
of oak-chip embers. I had thought he intended to cook over the
second fire. He now took several handfuls of crushed corncob
and scattered them into the tiny flames. Soon, a very thick
cloud of smoke was rising from the burning cobs. We inverted
the pot over the small pile, and left it to smoke inside. Only
nearly invisible wisps that escaped under the rim gave any indication of the contained smudge fire.

While the corn smoke did its mysterious job, we shared cups
of the now familiar tea. Since the leaves had begun to fall, Joe
was adding the crushed ends of sassafrass twigs to his brew.
These ends held the baby buds, which would bring the new
leaves to the trees after winter. I don't know whether the addition of the buds did it or not, but the stuff was beginning to
taste good. He explained that depending on the season, there
were always different types of illness to be guarded against. It
was fortunate that the Maker had provided the appropriate
remedies for each time of the year. It was no accident that the
spring brought new, soft shoots from the sleeping skunk cab-
bages and fresh buds from the slippery elms. The new roots of
the jack-in-the-pulpit plant were also important. The early cattail stalks with hard, green fruits were very useful, too.

By the time summer was in full force the leaves of certain
trees and plants were to be picked and dried for the coming

winter. These must be collected at the right time so they would be most potent. At this season the seeds must be taken from green apples, for they played an important role in sickness prevention. The pits of peaches and wild plums were to be saved.

When autumn colored the green leaves yellow and orange, it was time to begin collecting all sorts of herbs, leaves, roots, and berries, for soon there would be no more.

In winter there were still items such as the sleeping buds from many species of trees that could be gathered, but these could not provide all the needed ingredients. If one had not prepared for winter it was very possible that he might never see spring. Winter, he said, was the resting time. The time when the Maker had decreed most things should sleep. The bear went into her cave, not to emerge until the warming gusts told her it was time to give birth to cubs. The leaves fell, the green went away, and even the roots slept. Winter was the time to have all things near one, as did Hannick, the squirrel. The Maker had ordained that the rabbit and some other game should still be available, but these were only the means to provide a little extra food. What was in the wigwam when the snow began to fall was generally all one could really depend upon.

Joe's discourse on remedies and roots, seasons, and especially winter, brought all sorts of questions to my young mind. I knew certain things after several years of Boy Scout training, and I decided to ask about the conflicting ideas.

I asked Joe why he spoke of bears when anyone knew that there were no bears here to sleep their winters away. He agreed that the bears were all gone now. He said, a bit sadly, that there had been bears here once though. The Maker had always seen to it that there were bears in the old time. Konoh, the bear, was a very important animal to Joe's people. The skin of Konoh was the finest blanket that a brave could provide for his family. This skin would make it possible for them to sleep in the wigwam even if, by chance, the heating fire should die on a cold winter night. The teeth of the great bear were a medicine thing that would protect the bear's hunter as long as he wore them. The fat of the great animal was used in cooking and as a salve against insect bites or sunburn. It was even possible for a young Indian to enter the state of manhood in the eyes of his father and his tribe by hunting and killing the bear. In the old time, the skull of the bear had always been saved after the kill. It was cleaned and then painted. The totem object, for that is what it was, full of medicine, was placed on a stick near the home. By doing this, the hunter was protecting his family from enemies, hunger, and sickness. Yes, he said, the bear was surely a part of the great plan the Maker had used in providing for His people.

The bear was not angry with the hunter who was finally able to slay him. He knew that he had been sent here to be of use to an Indian family. He required only that his killer be brave and worthy. If the hunter was not, the bear was triumphant. It was in this way, among others, that the Maker had tested His children.

I asked him why, if the bears were important, were there none here anymore. His answer, sad in itself, has always stayed in my mind as a symbol of great loss.

"The bear is gone now," Joe Two Trees said, "because the Maker must feel no one is left who could respect him. None of His people need a blanket to warm them. None are worthy enough to wear the great teeth around their necks. None are left."

I reminded him that he was still here, and the Maker must surely take that fact into account in His great plan. He answered in a very solemn tone and posture. His reply made me hope that I would not someday be given the distinction of being the last of my kind. "The Maker has forgotten me. All of the people are no more, and only I am left here for a little while. Although I tried to learn the proper ways, it was already too late in the time of my father and mother. I am not Indian anymore. I am not white man. I am not worthy enough to hunt the bear. The Maker has forgotten me. Long ago He gave me a bear, but He took it from me later on. That once, I was an Indian again."

We sipped our tea for a long while in the silence of falling dusk. After a time we looked at the inverted pot, and Joe said the smoke fire still had to burn underneath. I decided to leave and return in the morning. The sky was struck with colors of gold, purple, red, and ocher as I walked my path toward Throggs Neck. The crickets had begun to count the passing seconds with their chirp. The air was very clean and quiet. I found it hard to believe that Tchi-Manitou had forgotten Joe Two Trees.

The morning finally came. When the other members of my family were still sleeping soundly, I gathered a few things and headed for my new pot, and my new friend. The walk seemed endless, and I imagined that the clay had cracked. I was sure that the whole thing had been too simple. I would find a crumble of burnt clay over a pile of burnt corncobs. The Maker could never place His sanction on the efforts of a young white boy.

I arrived in the campsite at the hour when darkness and light are still fighting to see which should prevail. I thought it was too early, and that the Indian might still be sleeping behind his bark walls. As I stood, trying to decide if I should wake him, I became aware of his presence behind me. I turned and he was there. I remember thinking quite often that it was not possible for a man to move as silently as he. I was often surprised like that, and I'm sure it was usually unintended.

The man asked if I would share his breakfast. Since I had left home so early, I was hungry. I asked if we could examine my pot, but he replied that the light was not good yet for such critical things, and so we ate.

Joe had not expected my company, and had prepared a meal for himself alone. He brought out an extra plate and poured some ground corn porridge into it. Next he scraped a dark mixture of sun-dried raisins, crushed hickory nuts, and tiny pieces of diced, smoked meat over the hot corn. The mixture was every bit as good as any breakfast I had ever eaten at home. He told me his name for the dried mixture, but over the years I've forgotten. I have read, though, that Indians made such a mix to bring along on hunting trips. It was light in weight, nutritious, and easy to carry in a small pouch. It is called "pimekan." This may also have been the Indian name I heard that day.

We finished our meal and by then the sun had beaten back the darkness. He said we could examine the clay piece now. We picked it up and he tapped it firmly with a small stick. He struck it on each side as he rotated it with one hand. This was to be sure it had no cracks or imperfections. If each tap had not had the proper sound it would have indicated a flaw. To my great relief, each strike rang true.

I examined our creation inside and out. The interior walls were coated with a moist, black covering. I rubbed at it and found that although the color came off on my fingers, the clay was permanently impregnated. Smoke from the corncobs had gone into the material itself and it was what now made the pot waterproof. I ran to the nearby spring and washed the soot and ash from the new utensil. When it was clean I filled it with water and set it in some grass. I wanted to test it and see for myself that water would not turn it back into soft clay. Joe, who had been watching me, laughed. He said I could trust this new pot because it had been made in the old way.

3

How "Medicine" Came to Be

After my excitement over the adventure of the pot had subsided a bit, I thought back to our conversation about herbs and remedies. I asked whether all the things he had mentioned, the roots, leaves, berries, and seeds, went into his tea at some season. He seemed surprised, and said that they did not. Some of the medicinals could make one sick if boiled in water. Others might even kill a person. He explained that by grinding certain roots and making a paste, he could cure mosquito bites. By boiling special leaves and then applying them to an infected wound, he could drive out the swelling. By chewing the right roots he could alleviate a toothache. To be sure, many of the plants could be used in tea, but not all. Each, however, used properly had its own purpose and effect.

Then he told me a story his father had told him about how Tchi-Manitou, the Maker-of-All, had taught His people to use herbs and leaves for medicine. In this way they could save themselves from the terrible sicknesses that often afflicted them.

The Creator called one man from each tribe, and He gathered them to learn the making of medicine. He showed them the proper herbs, leaves, stones, fruits, and internal organs. He taught them how these must be collected, preserved, and used. He explained the remedy that would help each different illness, and He told the Indians the mystical words that must often accompany these. Sometimes, He said, certain dances or other traditions must also be observed in conjunction with the medicine water or medicine salve.

Now He instructed each in the preparation of a very special mixture. Each was to use this only when all else failed, for it was powerful with great magic. This formula was to be guarded above all other things, and its secret told only to that person who would replace its holder as medicine keeper, upon death. The Maker told them that He would guard all their lives to be sure they would not die suddenly. In this way He enabled them to have time to pass on the secret. He demanded that they never let this medicine be used up, or its secret lost. On the day that this medicine was no more, the Indian people would vanish from the Earth forever, He told them.

With that strong warning, the Maker sent each man back to his tribe to be a hereditary medicine man. Joe thought there had still been such a person during his grandfather's life. His own father had not known the secret of the medicine, however, and before he died, gave his son the only thing left to him—the small supply of tribal medicine that remained. Joe showed me a small, clay jar with a plug of melted wax sealing it. This was all that was left.

He didn't know if it still retained any potency after all these years. I think he was afraid to find out. He was sure though, that the Maker's prophecy was soon to be fulfilled. His people would be gone forever.

He asked again, that day, if I would hear his story, so his memory would linger after his spirit had made its way across the stars. This seemed very important to him, and I agreed for the second time. Just as he had done the first time, he quickly changed the subject, and we spoke of other things. I thought it might seem impolite for me to remind him, so I did not. It was to take three askings before Joe actually undertook the telling of his origins and the deeds of his life. I don't know whether the number three had any significance to other Algonquins, but as time passed I learned that it had some magical connotation for Joe. Things that occurred in threes, or multiples of three, were always omens or signs for him.

I kept thinking about this story, and wondering if it would ever come. As the months passed, Joe told me many stories. He seemed to enjoy the telling of stories, and he was certainly very good at it. Often, he would wink and smile, saying he had a short tale if I wished to hear it. Once, I pointed out that the Great Spirit might become angry with us for telling stories during the summer. Joe, after all, had warned me that winter was the only proper time to tell stories. He grinned and said that these were no longer the old times, and he was sure the Maker would overlook the telling of a relatively unimportant story. He also predicted, quite accurately, that this winter might be his last, and stories untold would never be told again. I was sad to hear him say this at the time, but with the bliss of youth upon me, I felt quite sure he was mistaken.

So, during those waning days of summer in 1925, Joe found it excusable for many reasons to tell me all sorts of stories. He also made time to instruct me in any of the ancient ways that seemed to interest me. He said it was good that I learned Indian ways, for "being Indian" should not be lost completely.

4

A Gift Is Passed
Across the Ages

In those days my only sources of information about Indian lore were the local public library and the American Museum of Natural History, both of them frequent sanctuaries for me on rainy days. Based on the exhibits in the Museum, I made mental notes of projects I would like to try. High on my list was the making of an arrowhead, and it was while doing this under Joe's direction that I got to see the arrowhead pouch and other hereditary things left to him by his father.

Under Joe's guidance, I had just finished chipping finger grips in a large stone so it could be used as a hammer for flint. As I finished chipping, Joe disappeared into his small wigwam shelter. The door flap had been left ajar, and I could see that he was rummaging around inside. After moving several blankets and other paraphernalia aside, he began to dig at the edges of a flat stone that was embedded in the soil. After more prying and digging he finally loosened one corner of the rather large stone. Placing a sturdy pole under that part, he managed to lever the rock out of its clay mortar. Having accomplished this, he pushed the stone cover, for that is what it was, aside, and peered into the hole below. The tiny vault was lined with stones and made a very nice cache. He seemed a bit undecided as he kneeled there, but soon he reached inside and withdrew a pouch about the size of a lunch bag. He took the bag and weighed it in his hand. I could tell he was thinking about it in very serious terms. Finally, he came to some conclusion. Turning, he brought the pouch into the light of day.

We both looked at the still-closed pouch. I, with a kind of awe; he with a sort of reverence. It was of leather, and from its appearance very old. The material was a chestnut brown and quite stiff. It was creased and cracked open in several spots. The best description I can offer is that it had the look of age, very great age.

Here, Joe told me the story of the hidden cache. When he was just a baby and his mother still carried him in a pouch attached to a board on her back, men had come to this woods and discovered his father's presence. (This was probably during the early 1840s.) They frightened the father and mother into running to the mainland, on the other side of Vagabond Bay. The men had plans to use his father's home as a farm.

The father knew that he must leave or the men might kill his child and wife. He also knew that making a farm here would not be a practical job. The giant trees and deep-seated rocks would see to that. He felt that, in time, he would be able to return to this, the place of his father and grandfather. So he opened up the special hiding place that had been built by his great-grandfather, and secreted away all the medicine things. He hid the pouch, and other items of hereditary importance under the same heavy stone that his great-grandfather had used during the time of the Iroquois invasions. He removed all signs that this had been his camping place, and left with his little family.

In time, the stones and stumps proved more than the white men wished to move, and they left. The father came back across Vagabond Bay with his family. He was older, the baby was now a boy, the squaw had much silver in her hair of black, but the father could return to the land of his ancestors. Today, said Joe, was the first time the hidden vault had been opened since it was sealed by his father long, long ago.

He opened the pouch very gently and brought out the contents on a patch of soft grass. First came a portion of deer antler with two small tines protruding from it. I could tell that it was some sort of tool at a glance. The points, or tines, were worn and scratched. The handle portion was smoothed in a way only many years of use can cause. Joe said it was used in flaking the final point and edges on stone tools such as arrow-heads, knife blades, and spear points.

I was amazed to think that the deer that had once worn the antler had walked the woods of this very island. I was even more engrossed by the evident fact that the deer had been killed by Two Trees's great-grandfather, probably with an arrow tip of his own making. I began to feel very new to this world around me. I suppose I was, only then, beginning to comprehend the fact that things had been going on here for a very long time. Somehow, this thought was a reassuring one. I found pleasure in the idea that there was a continuity operating here, and I was part of it.

The next things out of the leather bag were objects of great beauty: flint, quartz, argillite, chert. They were all worked into arrow points and other edged tools. The Indian said we would use them as our models. When our abilities began to fail us we would fall back on the silent teachings of his ancestors.

In the old time, the making of these stone tools was an important thing for all braves. The man who did not become proficient in this skill was not able to kill the deer or bear. He was apt to go hungry much of the time. No woman of any intelligence would find him suitable for a husband. Nor would her family. So, young men sometimes made a small number of excellent stone tools and put them aside to save. These were not used in woodworking or hunting. When the young man found a girl he wanted for a wife, he would present these, along with other gifts, to her father. If the father was impressed with the man's work, he was more likely to feel favorably toward the marriage.

These particular tools had been made by his grandfather. They had been presented to his great-grandfather in order that he might smile on the courting of a daughter.

Over the years, the need for them had diminished. The Europeans brought knives of iron and guns for hunting. Finally, no one had tried to make the stones anymore. These, he said, that had been buried for so long, were simply "left."

On my way home that evening, I perched, for a short while, on Glover's rock to watch the sun fade. Looking toward Turtle Cove, I could almost convince my eyes that a dug-out canoe cut quietly across its smooth water. I knew it wasn't, but I thought, in the Maker's great plan it was there only yesterday. I didn't want to think what tomorrow might bring to this beautiful little place.

Joe Two Trees had once taken me to this cove. He had described the way the tribe, in his grandfather's years, would hide in the tall bulrushes from the ducks and geese. In fall, the birds would gather in flocks on the water. When they were tightly packed into "rafts," dozens of arrows would fly. The birds that were hit would be gathered with canoes, and brought home to the pot.

The ducks still come to Turtle Cove, but their aboriginal hunters have long ago perished.

The next morning I took the long way to Joe's camp, picking up pieces of flint as I went. When I reached the place at the top of Hunter Island, my pockets were bulging. I had high hopes for a successful making that day. But after what must have been fifty unsuccessful tries, Joe said a story was called for. When things went badly, it was sometimes wise to lay them aside for a time and rest the problem. What better way than by clearing the mind with a story? I agreed that things seemed to be going badly indeed. School would begin soon, summer was over, and my arrowheads were not to be ready in time to show them off.

Two Trees asked what I called the coming season; the time when the leaves began to fall and the corn and squash came ripe. He wanted my name for that time of year with frost at night but warm, summery days. I answered that we called it Indian summer. He seemed pleased that he had been able to lead me into giving him the answer he wanted.

During the hot days of summer, work must be done. It is then, he continued, that the crops must be watered and weeded. That is the time for hunting deer, for the hot sun's rays will help dry the strips of flesh for winter use. It is this season that sees the fish in their abundance. These should be caught and also dried for winter. Yes, in the great plan, the Maker made summer to be a season of work; just as He made winter to be a season of preparation. In winter, we weave nets, make fish spears, and construct bows. In winter, he said with a crooked grin, we make arrowheads for the hunting times ahead.

But there is an in-between time. Before the snows blanket the land, before the icy breath of winter has frozen ponds and streams, the Maker gives His children a last chance to harvest the corn, and prepare.

Now is the time that He calls to the spirit of sun to make his crooked walk across the sky. No longer can he sleep his dark times in the northern regions. He must now begin his journey low across the horizon. Soon, the Maker orders, he must sleep in the South until the gentle breath of spring stirs summer back to life.

The sun spirit knows this is true, for it has always been this way. But he asks permission to confer with Earth, the mother, and give her his instructions for the time that he will not be near. Great Spirit grants the request, and the council of two, Earth and Sun, meets on a mountain. Sun tells Earth, as he has done since the beginning, not to fear when the cold winds freeze her lands. He reassures her that he will watch, even while he walks the crooked path. He says she will soon know his warmth again. He will be back to bring the green, young shoots from her soil, and the leaves to her bare trees. Earth's spirit mother is first frightened, then reassured. She knows that her time of growing is done and now is the time for rest. She listens to Sun and believes that he will come again to melt her icy bonds.

Seeing that his job is done, Sun lights his pipe and allows its smoke to make warm clouds to blanket the land this last time. After this, he says, the clouds will bring cold snow, but this once they will still be warm.

Now he begins his crooked walk, and each day it brings him farther away. Although he strains his powers to make his rays reach back, it grows colder. Winter comes.

It is during the time of the council of two that the Great Spirit stays the progress of his seasons. It is the time during this council that He gives His children a short while more to prepare. This is why it has come to be called "Indian Summer."

Only after many years did I realize that the old man had told me the story in order to stop my sadness over summer's end. I discovered, much too late, that most of his stories had an importance hidden in them, as well as a simple entertainment value. I've forgotten so many of his stories, and those I remember may not be precisely as he told them anymore. I wish now that I had placed less value on other things, and learned more from the hermit storyteller.

He said that since a few days remained of my vacation, we should renew our efforts on the arrowhead. This time, I found it much easier to create my first flake. I made very few "scrapers" before I had a fine flake to work down. The flake began to take a new form. Soon it was roughly the shape of a Christmas tree in outline. I could see that it was thicker than the models from the pouch, and its edges were not sharp enough. I knew that any further blows with the large hammer stone would only do damage. I didn't know what the next step should be. Was the magical creation of arrow points still to be the provenance of Indians alone?

Joe reached into the old pouch and brought out the deer antler. Now, he said, hold the handle and feel it in your hand. Let it find a position that suits it. If you do this, it will work better when you begin to use it. I moved it around in my palm for a while, and its smooth shank soon seemed to be almost a part of my palm.

Joe took my arrowhead and examined it closely. He placed it back in my hand and indicated a small ridge on the edge near its base. Here, I was to push the point of the antler against the dark stone, on an angle toward the middle. I did, and was rewarded with a very small, thin flake. I placed the antler point a bit higher along the edge, and a second flake sheared off. I continued along the same edge toward the tip. Soon the edge had begun to be a blade. I ended the side with tiny flakes, bringing the tip to a neat point. Next, the other side was flaked in the same way. I had learned the technique called "pressure flaking."

The base part, the "stem" of the original Christmas tree, was still a bit lopsided. The man said we should examine the models from his pouch and decide how we would finish ours. Some of the tips were deeply notched on their bases. Some had a fishtail-type bottom. A few had no notching or base at all. Those were triangular. They didn't seem very practical since they would certainly be hard to attach to the arrow shaft. I mentioned that to the Indian and he agreed. He said he didn't know how they had come to be in his great-grandfather's possession, since they appeared to be Iroquois war tips.

That day I learned the purpose of the triangular tips which, many years later, I was to excavate among the bones of a young Algonquin boy. The old man explained that I was right in thinking this type would be difficult to keep on an arrow. It had not presented any great problem to the original users, though. The heads were wedged into a small split in the head of the arrow. A bit of pine pitch and a thin strip of bark held them in position. They were only meant to be used once.

When the arrow had found its mark in the body of an enemy, the Iroquois would pull out the wood, leaving the stone in the wound. In the event that the target had not been killed and ran away, the arrow tip in his flesh would ensure an infecting wound that would finish the job slowly.

Yes, in the old time the enemy had many tricks. It was possible that these very tips had, long ago, been taken from the bodies of Algonquins. Then, when his great-grandfather had been a young warrior, the Algonquin and Iroquois tribes were still at war. Joe thought it almost funny that these two ancient enemies had finally been forced into a friendship by the European conquerors.

Had our situations been reversed I might have found it hard to understand why the Great Spirit had not taken better care of His children. Even at that age, I was able to see the tragedy of the Indian race. Had I been cheated of my ancestral land, forced further and further from my way of life, and even murdered, my religious strength might have been shaken. Had I found myself alone, a hermit of the woods, last representative of a once great people, I might have wondered about my Tchi-Manitou. It was typical of this man, however, not to wonder at those things that happened to him. Certain events simply took place. It was not his station to do anything more than adapt and continue on. I don't think Joe ever doubted his Maker, later to reject the doubt. He simply never doubted at all. This man felt all things were a part of His great plan. Even if he could see no logic at times, that was because he was a child. The Great Spirit was the father and Joe could only obediently follow. One might say that his situation allowed no other choice, but that would overlook the fact that Joe had never really wanted one. The woodlands that his Maker had provided, the meager life He allowed, were things the Indian appreciated in every fiber of his sick old body.

Certainly there were hardships. The sicknesses came more often and stayed longer now that he was old. Sometimes it was very lonely, and Joe would wish that another had been the last, instead of him. Occasionally, he would stand near the grove of pine trees, late at night, to listen for a voice in the sighing wind. He might hear his father among the sounds of the pine boughs, calling him to another place. He might hear his mother telling of a hunting ground far away, where a wigwam had been made ready for him. Often, in loneliness, he would go to the old places of his tribe. He would try very hard to see images in his mind of how these places had been in the other time. As he got older, these things seemed to occupy a greater part of his time. There was only the small, white boy. Perhaps he was the reason the Maker wanted Joe to continue. The man knew that he was very old now, but if the great plan would use him to teach and train the boy, so be it. Maybe this was the way of the Great Spirit, to see that all things Indian should not be utterly forgotten.

5

"Indian Fishing"

The next day Joe asked if I would like to go fishing. Knowing I
was about to learn something new, I eagerly agreed.

We went down to the water, Joe carrying his bone-tipped
harpoon rolled into a reed mat. We stopped near a huge boulder
that sat perched upon an outcrop of bedrock. He told me that
the Indians used to sit on the rock and watch the fish enter the
enclosed marsh behind it. When they saw a school of many fish
go in they knew it was time to stretch their nets across the exit.

In later years the stone's name became Saxon Stone, but
since that day in a September of my boyhood I have always
called it Indian Rock. Many tides have washed past it over the
years, but it stands there still, a part of the history of Pelham
Bay Park.

Joe told me that he didn't climb the stone anymore. His eyes
found it hard to see the fish now, and his legs found it hard to
climb. But it was high tide, and with luck, the fish had found
their way into the little salt pond.

We unrolled the mat from Joe's spear handle, and inside was
a net made from bark fibers. We waded into the narrow chan-
nel, and Joe showed me a row of stakes driven into the mud on
each side of it. These were hidden in the tall grass, and appeared to be very old. I suspected that this was a place, like
Turtle Cove, that had provided many a meal in the "old time."

I watched him fasten the net to each stake on his side, and
did the same on mine. He then checked the bottom of the net

along its whole length, with his feet. Any obstruction holding the fabric off the bottom would provide an exit for the fish we sought. Finally, he was satisfied that all was ready. Now we could do other things while we waited for the falling tide to do its work.

He took some rather smelly pieces of clam from a small hiding hole under a stone. We baited two hand lines with it. The biggest fish, he said, were smart. They didn't enter the enclosed places. They would swim along the shore, sure of an escape route if danger should suddenly appear. These we would fool with our lines.

The hooks were very odd and deserve a description here. Each line terminated in a straight piece of bone about three inches long. They had sharp points at each end and were grooved in the middle. The line was attached at the groove. I've since learned that these are called gorges. Their method of action was that the bait would be swallowed with the gorge entering mouth and throat lengthwise. When the quarry turned to swim off, the gorge was pulled sideways, lodging itself. The fish was then pulled in, hand over hand. Study has shown that this was a very ancient fishing utensil which predated the invention of hook-shaped devices. My experience on that autumn day proved that the gorge could still work, even in the twentieth century.

While the tide went out through our net, and the baits waited for takers, Joe picked up his spear and we walked a little distance. He found a narrow creek where the waters of Vagabond Bay reentered Long Island Sound. He waded out to a submerged rock and stepped onto it. From that vantage, spear poised, he peered into the water. He stood so still that he seemed to have stopped breathing. He looked very much like the mannequins in the American Museum exhibits. He had become a part of the rock, a part of the water.

Suddenly, so quickly that my eye missed the motion, his arm drove the bone-tipped weapon under water. I could see that he was forcing it into a fish held against the bottom. Soon, he reached in and pulled out a striped bass of about ten pounds. He took it off his spear and threw it to me. My job was to scrape the scales off with my pocket knife.

I looked back and saw that one of the baited lines was taut

and vibrating. Soon I had two fish for scaling. The number continued to grow, and the net had not yet added its share. Scaling, I thought, was about to become my life's work.

Joe came walking back from his midstream station, carrying two more bass. One of the fish was so long that a good portion of its body dragged on the ground as it was carried. He added these to the general pile we had created by now. I was still keeping up with the scaling, but soon the pond would empty. Joe Two Trees looked first at the fish I had scaled, and then into the small pond, where hundreds of little fish darted, caught by the net. He said that although our catch was large, our numbers were small. We must now chase the young fish out through a small opening in the net, to swim the open water again. These would be the food for years to come. Just as we save the seeds of the corn for future plantings, he said, we would now plant fish for future catching. It was the way of the Great Plan.

He said we would gut our catch and remove their heads here. It would lighten the load, feed the crabs and raccoons, and leave less to dispose of later. This seemed sensible, but I remembered the fish heads that fertilized Joe's corn. I asked him what he would use in spring if we left the heads here. He replied that Joe Two Trees would plant no more corn. But as we cleaned the fish, I with my Boy Scout knife, he with a chip of flint, I found it very hard to keep up with the gnarled old hands of the fisherman. I felt in my heart that a person who was able to do so many things was not yet old. A man who had so much respect and love for his world could not possibly be ready to leave it.

When we finished we went for a swim in the rising tide to wash the fish from our bodies. Joe showed me how to use wet sand for a "soap." We dried in the breeze and lowering sun. Joe unrolled his reed mat and we piled the fish on it. We each gripped two corners of the mat and, stopping several times to rest our hands and arms, we eventually came to the poison-ivy-covered entrance to his home.

Joe said he would welcome my help if I thought I would not get into trouble by coming home late. I was sure it would cost me a talking-to, but I didn't mention that. We began splitting each fish along the backbone, he with stone, I with steel. Soon we were working by firelight. As an owl hooted greetings to the night from a nearby tree, we finished.

Now Joe dusted each fish with salt he had collected by evaporating seawater in the hollows of rocks. Then, piling them in a pyramid, he built a fire of soft, rotten apple, hickory and cherry wood in the center of the pile, covered it with his mat, and began to smoke the fish. After another day the fish would no longer be in danger of spoiling. They would now become a part of the winter stores.

We sat and watched the campfire dance with shimmering shapes. We listened to the sounds of night. The black-crested night heron passed over with a muted screech. A group of cicadas had begun their symphony in the trees overhead. It was a night that would be remembered for a lifetime, but lived only once.

The Indian asked me if my parents would not be worried. I lied; he knew I lied, but then said I should do what I felt best. I decided to stay and make my way home at early dawn. He brought tea from the bark hut and warmed it over the fire. We drank together and listened to the world of darkness. The entire universe was captured within our small circle of light. Reality could wait.

Joe Two Trees went into the hut again, and returned with the ancient pouch of leather in his hand. He held his grandfather's bride gift in the flickering light, and took up the few stones that connected his life to those before him. He placed them in my hand without a word. I sat and fingered the beautiful stones and then I asked why he had brought them out. "They are yours now," he said. "It is good that you should have them so that they may continue."

I couldn't believe he was giving me the pouch of arrowheads. I knew the man felt they were a part of all he had left. I knew the bag was his gold and silver. These were family heirlooms, passed across the generations. Ages gone were connected to this spot, this time, only by the pouch, but he chose to give it to a small boy. He said, "I know you can respect these things made by my people of long ago. Take them, that they may remain, and not be buried by the rain and snow. Keep them, and think, upon nights such as this, of their makers."

I could think of nothing to say in thanks, so I said nothing. I placed the leather pouch inside my shirt. It nestled against my flesh and made me shiver.

Far off, I heard a train whistle, and an owl hooted in reply. Crickets chirped a song while frogs tried to drown them out with basso profundo notes. A tiny sliver of moon rose from the east, and I watched it climb a cloudless sky. The stars were now eyes, watching over all creation. It must have been on such a night, I thought, that the Great Spirit decided to create all things. I asked Joe if he had a story about The Beginning. He had, and as the night shadows gradually thinned he told it to me—the story of how Sky Woman, the Earth Mother, brought her twin sons, Good and Evil, to the world; how they created the sun and the night; how they fought until Good wounded his brother and banished him to the nether regions from whence he sends up his helpers to make trouble on Earth. When he finished, the sky was light in the east.

"That was the story of The Beginning," said Joe. I tell it to you as my father told it to me."

"Do you believe it?" I asked him.

"I believe the story is as true as you want it to be. Is there more than that?"

I paid for that night away from home. My parents, worried, had not gone to bed that night either. Punishment was both swift and lingering. The swift part affected only the seat of my pants, but the lingering part was a prohibition that kept me away from my Hunter Island for many weeks.

During that time I told part of the Beginning story to my former 1A teacher, Miss Mellert, whose room I had gone to one day after school. She advised me to use every chance I had to read library books and other works on the Algonquins and Iroquois, and I did. I studied everything on the subject I could find. Trips to the museum helped, and soon the fall was turning to winter. A bit before Christmas my sentence was suspended. I promised my father that I would keep track of time in the future, and made my plans for the coming weekend.

Friday night was cold and windy. When I woke in the dim glow of Saturday morning, a thin layer of snow was covering the ground. I turned frequently to watch my footprints extend in a line toward Hunter Island. The early sun on this first snow of winter was bright and cheerful. I hardly felt the wind as it drove cold air into my coat and muffler. I had other things to think about. I couldn't wait to see Joe and ask him to verify some of the things I had read in the past weeks. I wondered what new projects he would help me undertake. I saw us walking together, looking at new things and telling strange stories to each other. I wanted to tell Joe all the things I had learned, for I knew he would be pleased with me.

It seemed longer than it usually was, but the path finally ended at the Indian's camp. I noticed there were no footprints in the snow at the entranceway. I thought it surprising since it was already late morning, and Joe was an early riser. Had he had no business outside of the camp? I went through to the inside. No fire burned; no signs of activity were evident. The compound was quiet and eerie.

I pushed aside the flap entrance to Joe's small shelter, and there he was, wrapped in blankets. He lay on his bed of pine branches and smiled at me weakly. I asked what was wrong and he said that he had been sick for many weeks. He had broken the wax seal on the medicine jar his father left, but it was all dried up and gone. He had grown very weak. I saw that Joe, like his medicine, had also dried up. He looked so small, lost among the blankets.

I hurried to start a small fire. This done, I boiled some tea in hopes the therapeutic ingredients might help the man regain his strength. He drank, and by early afternoon he seemed somewhat better. After a time, I helped him to a seat by the fire. I warmed up ground corn mixed with water, and he managed to eat a small bit. I could see plainly that any improvement he showed would only be temporary. I begged him to let me take him to a hospital in the city, but Joe laughed and said the city would only hasten his death. "I was born in the Maker's woods; this is where I shall die when He ordains it." I could feel that he was adamant as his flint, and knew he would want his wish respected. In any case, there was no way to transport him the many miles that would be required. I saw there would be no more makings, no more Indian craft projects, no more stories. But I was not completely right. The man asked me for the third time since I had known him if I would hear his story.

I told him it would be my privilege to do so. I would keep it always, telling my children when the time came, so that Joe would never really be gone from the woods he loved. He was pleased.

II

Joe Two Trees

JOE TWO TREES'S TRAVELS

Dates are approximate, but it is possible to estimate fairly closely from his story, and one can say fairly accurately that his sojourn away from Hunter Island covered about eight and one-half years.

 1 Hunter Island (see Map on page 2), where Two Trees was born in 1840, and where he lived until 1855, when he left for New York City.
 2 Manhattan, where he worked in the winter of 1855–1856.
 3 Staten Island, where he spent the summer of 1856.
 4 In the fall of 1856 he crossed from Staten Island into New Jersey.
 5 He camped in New Jersey during the winter of 1856–1857 and the summer of 1857.
 6 In the fall of 1857, he crossed Pennsylvania, camping there through the summer of 1858.
 7 In the fall of 1858 he arrived at the coal mine, and worked there for at least two years—into late 1860.
 8 It was probably during the winter of 1860 that Two Trees left the mine and made his way back into New York State.
 9 He stopped in southern New York State near the Hudson River in the late summer of 1861, and remained there until the early summer of 1862.
10 During the summer and fall of 1862 he was on the Hudson River, heading back to New York City, reaching it in the early winter of that year and remaining there for the rest of his life.

6

The Joining
of Two Clans

I had assumed that Joe and his people had always lived in
Pelham Bay Park and that the story would begin there. Instead, he began his story with Aquehonga, the water we call
Bronx River. That is where in the old time Joe's ancestors, a
clan of about ten related families, had lived. In the riverside
woods, they hunted the many deer. In the river they fished for
salmon, trout, and other fish that would come up from the
distant salt water. When summer came they would travel to a
fishing village far downriver. It was called Snak-a-pins. Here,
many clans would gather and make temporary homes. They
would collect shellfish and catch large numbers of black fish,
bass, mackerel, and even sturgeon.

At Snak-a-pins, clans and even tribes from the north, called
Siwanoy, would share the land and live peacefully. It was always a good time for the people. At night, clans that never saw
each other in winter would meet by the fires and exchange news
from different parts of the land. The nearby waters provided
food for all, and full bellies made for happy talk.

Here, many marriages were arranged. Families who in those
times had made strong friendships during the summer encampment often would encourage their children to tie bonds, joining
them in permanent alliance. A marriage at this place was also
thought to be a lucky one that would produce many offspring.

By day, the fishermen would take their canoes as far as Sewan-Hacky, across the water (Long Island's shore), and to

Monatun, where the waters run fast (Hell Gate). When night was coming, they returned with the catch.

From the beginning, Joe said, the people had met there each summer. It was a place, and time, of good medicine. Snak-a-pins had still existed when the first whites began to arrive. He had often wished it had been his lot to live then, when the people were still alive.

Things had changed, though, when the Europeans came. The clan had returned to Aquehonga one fall and found a new settler building a log house near their winter village. They talked to him during that winter, and by spring, the clan had accepted an offer from this new man. He showed metal knives, iron kettles, hatchets, blankets, shirts, and with these, the people reasoned they could make another home in the woods of a different place. The name of that man had been Jonas Bronck, whose purchase is documented in 1641.

The clan had spent the following summer at Snak-a-pins, but they knew they would have to find a new home in fall. No more would the high bluffs of Aquehonga echo with their children's laughter. They talked to many families, asking how the land was where they made winter wigwams.

One clan, related to Joe's ancestors through a marriage at Snak-a-pins, asked that the homeless people join them in a place near the holy rocks called Mishow. This was a place of many springs with good water, tall forests, and islands divided by fine waterways. The ducks and geese visited the shores in great numbers. Deer and bear were plentiful on the wooded islands. The clans agreed, and when autumn came, the two turned as one, toward Mishow.

After a walk of one day, they stood in the homeland of the new clan. It was a new clan, for now they were one. The spot where they would formally make the bonds was Mishow. These rocks stand, somewhat buried, but still visible today, near the parking lot at Orchard Beach in the Bronx.

It was now time to prepare wigwams for the new people. All worked together, and soon saplings were bent and frameworks built. The squaws wove mats of bulrush and cattail reeds. The frames were covered with these mats, and then with slabs of bark. A hole was left in the center of each new roof to allow the cooking smoke to find a way out. Flat stones were brought to cover the chimney holes, and the houses were soon ready. Other things still needed to be done, but the matter of shelter was accomplished. The other details could wait, for tonight would be a celebration. As with the marriage of two people, the joining of two clans called for ritual and feasting.

The corn was ready to be harvested. The crops, tended by those few who did not make the trip to Snak-a-pins each summer, were good this year. Many baskets would be filled with winter food when all began the picking, but now, enough was taken for a fine meal.

The children were sent to gather clams, oysters, mussels, and crabs on the low tide. Even lobsters fell prey to the young hunters.

Soon, the makings for a fine feast had been brought together near the holy rocks. Piles of firewood were prepared and every family busily gathered items for the coming festivities.

When evening came, all was ready. The fires were lit and the people began to gather in a large circle around the rocks. Soon the food was served, and all ate till their bellies were bulging. After everyone had eaten, the clan chief, or sachem, rose and walked to the rocks. He talked of welcome, and everyone said in unison, "It is good." The sachem spoke of the large number that now comprised the clan. He said that this would help them to ward off their enemies. He said that numbers also meant more mouths to feed, and ordered the people to be careful in their hunting, not to waste, to share with each other. Council would be held near these rocks to settle any disputes among the clan members.

The chief said that a clan as strong as this one should have a powerful name. There were many turtles in the woods, and along the shores here, and he would make a fine name for the new group. His strength held up the world, his name would strengthen the clan. He became the totem, their special animal symbol, their name. They were now the Turtle Clan.

When the fires began to burn low, the chief said that those who were from the old Mishow clan and the Aquehonga clan should stand two by two between the sacred rocks and embrace. This would show the Great Spirit they were now one family, all branches growing from the same tree. By the time they had done this the fires were out and all returned to their homes for the night.

The new group flourished and they did all the things their sachem had ordered on the night of the joining ceremony. They hunted and planted, fished and lived well. Some died, but new children were born often, and they stayed a large clan for many years.

During this time, in 1654, a man named Thomas Pell had come to live nearby. He wished to buy land here, and after the people saw that he was a good man who dealt honorably with his Indian neighbors, they agreed to listen to his offer of purchase. Although the Turtle clan was not directly involved in the transaction, their brothers on the mainland invited them to the deliberations. They were, after all, nearby, and this sale could well affect them too. Subsequent studies revealed many of the details of what followed.

The white man spoke to the Indian delegation for a long time. He promised peace and respect. He said he would interfere with their lives as little as possible. He told them that he would stay away from their holy places, and allow them to hunt on the land even after it was his. He promised the red men that he would use the land and its game in ways that would not anger their Great Spirit.

Joe's people listened in silence, and when he had finished, they walked off a little way to make council. After everyone had spoken, the leader saw that the agreement would be made. Now he must bargain for a high price. The beads and knives, jackets and pots had simply proven too much for the forest people to resist. The sale was made now; all that remained was a final price.

The Indians and white man sat down under a large oak tree that day and made treaty. A steatite smoking pipe was passed from hand to hand to seal the agreement. The Indian people with their new pots and beads and other treasures were very much poorer when they finally stood up.

The oak tree grew alongside Shore Road near the present Bartow Mansion. It grew there, a landmark from earlier times, in an open field until early in the twentieth century when it was struck by lightning. It subsequently died and rotted. Now, an iron fence stands around the spot where Thomas Pell pur-

chased Pelham Bay Park, parts of Westchester, and areas of the
Bronx in 1654. The final price must have been one of the best
bargains in history.

The treaty was otherwise a good one, and both sides lived by
it. But the seeds of the end had been sown with its signing. All
people who make treaties have one thing in common. None of
them lives forever.

By the early 1700s, the tide of immigrants from across the
sea was just beginning, and they all wanted land. They wanted
land to plant on, land to live on, land to buy and sell. Sometimes they acquired it fairly; sometimes questionably, often
they simply stole it, or killed the inhabitants.

First, with the new weapons, the white man killed all the
bear and deer on the island of Manhattan. What could possibly
follow except an exodus of the remaining Indians, who depended on the game for food and clothing.

Some of the clans and tribes went north and west to join the
old enemy, the Iroquois. Others crossed the Bronx and fled
through Westchester into Connecticut to ally themselves with
the Siwanoy. Some, in the more remote areas, simply stayed
where they were and hid. The time was one of great confusion.
It was the end, the breaking up of many strong tribes, the
scattering of the people.

The English had displaced the early Dutch, and it made little
difference that Americans would soon displace the English. All
had acted in unison on only one front, the displacement of the
natives. War was coming from a country-island across the sea,
but that was not important to the remnants of Indians who hid
in these woods.

The Iroquois came still, in those years, but they did not come
for slaves or tribute. They spoke of peace and of a prophet
whose name was Hiawatha. They explained the teachings of
this man, and their confederacy of five great nations. This
force, Joe said, was all that was left to defend the Maker's
people. They asked us as true Indian brothers to join them in
the north. Come, they entreated, and we will adopt you as our
own.

The woods became emptied of Indians. Even members of the
Turtle clan left in large numbers. A council was held at the
sacred rocks, and all those who were left spoke what was in

their hearts. There were no more great fires as there had been long ago. These would only alert the white enemy to the Indians' presence. "We were a hidden people, at a hidden council," Joe said.

They asked the Great Spirit to guide them in the right path; to give each family the plan best for it. They used great medicine words, words unspoken during all the years of peace. They brought forth amulets hidden for so long that none remembered their origin. These were times when only the strongest medicine might bring some answer, if answers existed at all.

"When the council ended," the old man went on, "only two families had decided to stay in the old places. These were the families of Long Canoe, my great-grandfather, and that of Torn Moccasin. Long Canoe had a wife, one son, and two daughters. Torn Moccasin had no wife, as she had died, but had two sons."

They made their parting that night, and all promised to see the others again. Long Canoe wished them well, and said that if the spirits did not decree their meeting again, he was sure that the Maker had prepared wigwams that would be close together for all of them to live as neighbors in the Happy Hunting Ground. When Long Canoe and Torn Moccasin awoke in the morning, the others were gone. The strong Turtle clan now consisted of eight people. During the winter, two of these were buried, having caught the spotted sickness of the whites.

7

Last of
the Turtle Clan

It must have been around that time that war broke out among the white men. Joe's father had told him of the day Long Canoe walked the shores at Turtle Cove. There he saw the great gathering of ships, said Joe. The red-coated soldiers covered all the beaches when that day ended. Joe was sure that Long Canoe had watched without knowing which of his many enemies were disembarking. Joe was also sure that he wouldn't have cared at all. One was as deadly as any other.[1]

During that war, the grandfather of Joe had been born. He was called Red Dawn, in hope that a new era would rise with him. He married one of the few remaining young girls, and she was Morning Flower. They had one son and called him Eagle Feather. Eventually Eagle Feather married the last Algonquin girl, Small Doe. They had a son and his name was Two Trees.

The name of the boy had been inspired by a small island, just off the shore of Twin Island, near Hunter Island. During the boy's youth it was crowned with bushes, scrub, and two strong trees. The island was small, and it was alone. I think I understand why Eagle Feather and Small Doe chose it to name their son.

Joe, for that is what I still called him, asked me to warm more

[1] Joe's knowledge of the Revolutionary War was probably scant at best, but he seems to have been referring to the landing made by British general Sir William Howe on the morning of October 12, 1776, with some 30,000 soldiers.

tea. I did, and he sipped it slowly. He seemed a bit better than he had earlier in the day. His eyes stared into the small fire, and I wondered what sights they might be seeing. He was remembering, and trying to visualize things he had never even seen. These were things that had been told to him as a story history of his people. The mind is very important to a people with no written language. He was recalling events that happened hundreds of years, or more, ago, in another time, another reality. I saw pain flicker across his features, and wondered whether it was caused by his illness, or what he saw amid the embers. He seemed to find the images he searched for, and the story continued.

He told again of the time his small family, last of the Turtle clan, had been forced away by the white men. His father had not been able to come back until Joe was thirteen seasons old. He counted these out for me on his withered fingers. Then his gaze found the opened medicine jar only recently taken from the stone cache. Reminded by his thoughts, he regarded it wistfully for a moment.

During the time on the mainland, Eagle Feather had made short trips at first. He looked for other Indians. Over the years, his trips had lasted longer. Finally, he had wandered around their camp of exile and cried much of the time. He had faced the facts—he and his little family were alone. The father made no more trips. Instead, he spent his time instructing Two Trees in the Indian way. He spent hours each day, teaching the boy about his ancient heritage. At some point, the stories became Eagle Feather's life. He lived for the telling with Two Trees, the boy.

Then, one day the boy came back and told his father they could return to the old place. The men had gone. The island could be their home once more. They could go back to the land of the Turtle. The father seemed pleased, and they rolled their belongings into mats. Joe carried the bundles to the canoe and the family paddled across Vagabond Bay.

During the time of rebuilding the ancient camp the father seemed better. His spirit returned, and he worked with a will. But the building and preparing didn't last long. When the camp was again as it had been, the father walked all the woods of the island. Again, he was looking for Indian brothers. In time he knew he would find none, ever. He sat upon a rock, and refused to eat. Joe tried to feed him, but four days later he was dead.

There was no funeral ceremony as in the old times. No one was left to bid farewell except a young boy and an aged wife. Two Trees took his father and, in the old way, buried him. He did all the work alone to spare his mother the sorrow of burying the last initiated Algonquin brave. He put many things in the ground: a hatchet, a knife, a stone pipe. He also placed the shell of a turtle in the grave. The turtle would be strong medicine during the trip to another place. There would be many camping stops along the Milky Way before his father reached the floating island.

A thirteen-year-old boy and his very old mother were now the last of the Turtle clan. The boy sometimes wondered if Tchi-Manitou might have forgotten that even they were left. He did what he could to make life easier for the old woman, but she was sick most of the time. Joe made tea and used the herbs and leaves. He tried all the remedies that had worked well in the old time, but nothing seemed to improve her. As hard as he tried, he knew he was losing her. She spoke bravely, and she counseled him not to worry over her, but each day saw her moving toward Eagle Feather. One morning, when winter was fighting off the advance of spring, Joe could not wake Small Doe. She had gone to join her husband. She had left her son behind.

The mighty Turtle clan had come to this. One man was left to bury his mother. One name was left to walk the old paths, to hunt the old places. One man was left to hear the sighing pines speak, and ponder the glow upon the Milky Way. He was fifteen years old.

The man-boy did all the things that had become his routine. He tended the crops and hunted the dwindling game. He caught and dried the fish, and put the meat up for winter. He mended the wigwam shelter in expectation of cold winds to come. He hid from any passing eyes, and cowered in fear a great deal of the time. He took to waking very early, to walk the shores and hills before any other would be stirring.

When winter came he was confined to the small hut for great

lengths of time. The snow seemed much deeper than when his parents had been alive to joke about his fears. He heard many noises in the night and was often sure they were to be his end. The days, watching a tiny fire, went very slowly. That winter Joe learned of loneliness. It was a predatory beast. It stalked him in the dark places. It waited just at the wigwam flap for him to come out. The beast hid behind every rock, every tree. It lived in all the places where laughter used to dwell.

This was a very bad winter for Two Trees, and on occasion he thought of suicide. Then, a warm day would come to chase the cold away and Joe would decide to wait for the fawn to bring summer. So it went through January and February. March brought days when the boy thought summer must surely have come, only to have them smashed with sleet or snow. But, after a very long season, green buds started to burst into leaves. Joe began to walk more now, and the pink apple blossoms kindled the embers in his heart. The fear left his spirit, and he was reborn with the new birth of spring.

During summer he did the things Eagle Feather had taught him. He worked at the corn, beans, and other crops. He prepared and put aside for the coming winter. He repaired the wigwam and made new traps and snares. He would often swim and wash himself with clean, wet sand. The fear was not gone, though; it still waited to trap him in the shadows of evening. He held it away with industrious work. He was preparing as he had done during every summer of his young life, for the winter to come.

Fall came, and Two Trees awoke one day to the knowledge that he must now pick the corn. He had waited this long only because he didn't want to acknowledge the loss of summer. He wasn't looking forward to the winter that would shortly come.

Joe picked the corn and beans; he picked all his crops. He had soon put away a good store for the cold time. He stocked and prepared during the Indian summer, and when winter came, he was ready. His mother's baskets and clay jars were full to overflowing. The shelves were heavy with smoked fish. The firewood was piled outside his hut. Many nuts were stored in stone-lined holes around the campground. He slept, surrounded by his provisions.

8

The American City— New York

Early the next morning Joe put on his leather trousers and shirt, washed his face at the spring, and left. He walked toward the white man's city. These were not his people, but at least they were people. Joe wanted a human voice. The language was unimportant. He would learn their words. He was ready to join the new men, on their terms, just to be included again among human beings.

At first he walked among the woods and hills that he had always known; but when he reached the mainland, the trees began to thin. Now and then he passed farms and buildings. Soon the road became a broad street, and he began to see people. First one, then two or three, and finally many. They looked at the boy in strange ways, as though they couldn't imagine what, or who, he might be. Two Trees walked faster, trying to avoid any contact. He knew it must come, but it frightened him. The people wore strange clothing, and looked very different from him. Maybe this was the reason they peered after him as he passed. The boy was afraid, but his resolve was strong. He felt this fear among other men. The fear that waited back at his island was fear alone, fear that would grow, during the winter, to become a terrible beast and devour him.

He walked at a brisk pace in a direction where he could see smoke rising into the sky. The white man's village must be large to have so many campfires. The streets were different here. They were paved with square stones. Now large wagons rumbled over the stones, pulled by teams of horses. People were everywhere here, and all were rushing to and fro. The boy thought this must be a harvest, or something like it. Everyone carried boxes or bundles from one place to some other, and returned to get the next one. Piles of boxes were built in a certain spot, only to be dismantled and hidden inside wagons. Then new wagons would come, and their contents would be made into piles where the others had been. It was very confusing. The boy tried to understand, but the purpose of all this work eluded him. He could recognize, though, that it was work, and Two Trees was no stranger to that. He stood and watched until the system began to form a pattern. Each man carried when ordered to by one who stood on a platform and made marks on a paper. The buckskin-clad boy watched until he was sure he had made no mistake. The man with the paper was boss. Two Trees was sure now. He knew that a boss could pay for work done. He would make the boss understand that he wished to work for pay.

He started toward the platform, but then, abruptly, everyone stopped working. The boss said a few words to the men and walked into a large building. The workers all picked up coats from a pegged board at the platform's end, and left.

Joe was disappointed that he had not been able to join the workers. He walked around the vicinity for a while, to familiarize himself with the strange streets and alleyways. It was beginning to get dark now. He would need to find a spot to camp, and quickly.

He rounded a corner and looked down the long street ahead of him. Something amazing had happened here. On a tall pole at each corner burned a tiny fire. He stopped and watched one for a long time. It flickered and flared, but he could not tell what it was burning. He noticed that the light did help him to see things better, though. He shrugged his shoulders at the strange occurrence and walked on.

Later, he found an alley between two dark buildings. At the end of it he could see the outline of trees. This would serve as well as any other place of the city, thought the youngster. He walked into the deep shadows, and dogs began to bark nearby. He stood still and soon they stopped. He reached the end and saw that it was a good place. If danger should come from the street, he could escape between the trees. Scraping together a mound of leaves, he sat and listened to the strange sounds of white man's night. A dog barked, a cat screeched, a wheel ground against stone, a man yelled, a door slammed; the boy huddled into his nest of leaves.

Hunger began as a persistent pressure in his belly, and it pulsed stronger as the minutes passed. He hadn't eaten since the previous night, and now he was becoming aware of it. He took some maize bread and a bit of dried fish from his pouch, and ate. Water stood in a small puddle nearby, and he drank. He reflected that on the next day he had better find paying work, for the pouch would not provide many meals.

Tired from the long walk the boy soon dozed, but he woke every few moments. New sounds and strange smells assailed the forest boy, and sleep would not overcome his senses.

At that time when the shadows are deepest and night is at her darkest, the boy stood up. Some infallible clock, born of years under an open sky, told him that gray would soon appear in the east. He put everything back as it had been and walked to the street. He looked back and made certain no sign remained of his encampment. He wanted this place to remain his secret. He felt he might use it for a long time.

He walked to the street where he had watched the men move boxes. When the eastern light had only begun to chase the dark, he saw the man who was boss walking toward the platform. The Indian ran up to him, and with many signals and pantomimes made his case for a job. The man seemed pleased. Two Trees didn't know it but the day was Sunday. The boss knew that after a holiday, a full work crew seldom showed up. He told the boy to come back the next day and work.

When the other men arrived, the boss said some words that the boy couldn't understand, and all began to move boxes. The Indian hurried to join, and soon he was part of the general confusion. The workers often laughed at him and said, "Indian Joe," but he laughed with them. Soon, he had a new name. Now he was Joe. He was pleased when he understood that this was a white man's name.

Joe worked hard and the boss hardly yelled at him. He arrived earlier, and moved more boxes than the others. When the lunch break came, the men would often give him bits of food from their meals. They taught him words, and his young mind learned them quickly. After six days, the boss told him the next day was no work. He handed Joe three silver dollars, and told him to come early on Monday.

Joe went walking to find a store. He was hungry and had money to pay for food. He wanted to find a place to buy corn, or beans or maybe even fish, but all the stores were closed. At last he passed a window and saw people sitting at tables, eating. Joe entered and sat at one of the many tables. He didn't know much about restaurants, but he knew that money was in his leather pouch. A woman came and Joe finally understood that she wanted to know what food he would have. He became confused. He showed her the three dollars, and then he remembered a word the men had taught him. "Sandwich," he told the woman. Time passed and she brought a cheese sandwich, and took Joe's three dollars. He tried to complain, but knowing no words, he took the woman's arm and tried to grab the money. A big man ran up and pulled at Joe. When he turned, the man hit him. Then the man threw Joe out the door onto the hard street. The door opened again, and the man threw the sandwich at Joe. The boy could hear cruel laughter behind the door as he picked up the parts of his sandwich.

Joe took the food and walked toward his alley. It was Saturday night, and music came from many doors. People laughed and drank beer, talked, and enjoyed the eve of their day off. The boy was not a part of any merriment.

When he came to his alley hideaway, he took the flint knife from inside his shirt and carefully cut the sandwich into six pieces. These would be his meals during the week to come. Tonight, he would not eat.

Sitting in his little den of leaves, he held his knife and watched the way light glinted from its edges. Each chip was a tiny facet giving the long blade a sparkling life of its own. Eagle Feather had made the knife. Joe pressed its hard side against his cheek and tried to make it help him remember the old time. It was good having his father's knife. The hard stone was a link between the now and the then. He fell asleep with the Indian knife resting on his face.

He woke early and set out to explore. Around the outskirts of the city he found fields with scallions and wild carrots growing. He filled an empty stomach with these, the things he knew. He took some and filled his pouch. At least he wouldn't starve. A sandwich, and these would assure it. Having made this new discovery he returned to the alley to put the roots on the ledge where he had left the sandwich.

From the mouth of the alley he could already see that something was moving near his spot. He ran into the shadows and saw a pack of rats scurry from the spot where his sandwich had been. Gone was the product of his first week's work.

Evening came, the boy ate some of his roots and slept. He woke early. He had had a dream, but it was gone now. When he first opened his eyes he had remembered it, but it soon was lost. He thought and tried to recall, but it was part of the dream world again. He thought it might have been about the old time, though, because it left him very happy.

With a smile on his face, he arrived at work. The camaraderie and activities of the day made him feel that he would find a place in this new world, a place for Joe. He worked hard, and the days passed. The men still gave him food at lunch, and at night he ate the roots from nearby vacant lots. He learned many new words, and by the end of that week he was able to say "I thank you boss" when he was paid.

It was Saturday night again, and three dollars were in the pouch. This time, thought Joe, he would be smarter. Taking two of the shiny coins, he buried them under the trees in his alley. This would be his store of money, just as his father had taught him to put aside a store of food. If hard times came, he would know he was prepared.

He took the single dollar and walked out to the street. Finally, he found what he wanted, a small general store. He looked through the glass, and a man sat within, playing music on an instrument Joe had never seen. Later, he discovered that it was a violin. Only a small lantern cast its feeble glow, and the boy thought the store was closed. He tapped hesitantly at the window, and the man looked up with a smile. He motioned the boy to enter and walked toward the door. When the man spoke, Joe realized that he, too, used these American words only as a newly learned tongue. The shopkeeper seemed unconcerned at Joe's odd clothing and this put the boy more at ease. He offered coffee, and the Indian accepted. It was a dark and bitter potion, strange to his mouth, but it was hot. He joined the man near an iron wood-burning stove and they drank.

With no small difficulty, they surmounted their language problems, and the man told of his country. His family were farmers in a place named Italy. Although they were poor they had saved enough money to send him to this new America. He had used the last of the money to buy this small store, and worked to save enough to bring his family here, too. Joe felt a warm kinship with the man. He too, had left his place to come to this strange city. The man said his name was Tony, and they each had found a compatriot.

The boy bought a round of cheese, a large loaf of bread, and several other items of food. Tony took the dollar from the boy's extended hand, and returned several smaller coins. Seeing the confusion on Joe's face, the man tried to explain "change." The boy didn't understand it all, but he learned that this Tony was an honest man.

The weeks passed, and the hidden store of money grew steadily. Each week Joe would buy his meager needs from the shopkeeper, and hide the rest of his pay. Tony and Joe would often sit, late at night, and puzzle over the strange ways of these Americans. Joe was the only one who had come from this land, but oddly, thought the two, no one saw him as an American.

During this time, Tony taught Joe the rudiments of counting and arithmetic. He sold the boy new clothes at prices that could only have been less than he had paid. He provided company, companionship, and maybe that was most important of all.

One Saturday, when Joe was finished work, and on the way to his alley with the pay, three men watched from a barroom across the street. They knew it was payday, and had spent all their own money. The three eyed Joe and sized him up as an easy mark. They slipped into the falling gloom and followed.

Joe had become confident in his routine. He worked, he visited Tony, and he went to the spot that had become home. No one bothered him. He had no reason to suspect followers. He was anxious to put the money in his spot, and then join Tony for coffee and talk. Joe didn't think to look behind him.

The men watched him enter the alley. This was perfect. If they had been able to choose their spot, they couldn't have chosen a better one. One of them circled to the building's rear, to cut off any escape. The other two entered from the street, with knives in hand. Joe saw these two, silhouetted against the dim gaslight.

The rock cover was off his money hole, and the men had seen it. He knew he could only fight now, flight was impossible. They would steal his stored dollars. He drew the flint knife from inside his coat, and stood ready to meet the two.

He braced in preparation for their attack, and suddenly pain shot through his shoulder. He hadn't seen the third man, the one who stabbed him from behind.

He turned, and instinctively drove his stone blade into the attacker. He caught the man at the center of his rib cage. Thrusting upward, the knife ripped into his heart. The man was dead before his body crumpled onto the hard ground. The only sound was a low, gutteral grunt as the flint had found its target.

The two others saw the body and quickly thought better of their plan for the easy mark. They turned and ran from the place, yelling for the police.

Joe had no time to think. He knew this place had served its final purpose for him. Scooping the dollars into his pouch, he fled through the trees. The last thing he heard was the barking of the dogs. He wondered, with a small part of his mind, if they were the same ones that had welcomed him to this alley six months before. The rest of his mind was occupied with one single thought. "What will I do now?"

Alone, in trouble, and afraid, he thought of his one friend, Tony. He quickly headed to the haven of his shop. The man was there. Seeing blood on Joe's jacket and sleeve, Tony brought him inside. He looked up and down the street and, satisfied that no one pursued, lowered the shades of his store.

The man calmed the Indian and helped to clean off the blood. He washed the shoulder wound and bandaged it with clean rags. It was deep, but it appeared a clean cut, and Joe was a strong, young boy. He would recover.

The boy said that now he was a brave, as his ancestors had been. He had killed his first enemy, and received a blood wound in the fighting. "Now," he said, "I am Joe Two Trees, warrior." Tony found little to make sense of in this logic. He told Joe that, brave or not, he must now flee to a place of safety. The men would identify him easily, and soon police would find him.

They would lock him in a metal cage and after some preliminaries, hang him from a rope until he was dead.

Joe protested that he had not struck first. He had killed the
man only to save himself and his dollars. Surely, they would
not hang him for this. The crime had not been his.

Tony laughed. He told the boy that the men would have
many friends. These would be the witnesses and jury at his
trial. Joe would have no one to speak for him except an Italian
shopkeeper, unsure of the language at best. His fate would have
been decided long before Joe saw the inside of a courtroom.

The boy eventually saw the truth of Tony's irrefutable words.
They agreed that he must now leave. Where he should go was
the next issue. Still firm in his hopes for a place in the white
man's world, Joe would not return to his island.

Tony had an uncle who had come to America years ago.
They had not seen each other since both had lived in Italy. The
uncle had written once that he owned a small farm at the end of
Staten Island. It had been years since Tony had heard anything
from this man, but it was all he could think of for the boy. He
told Joe his uncle's name, and making a rough map, explained
where he lived. Tony wrote a letter, in Italian, explaining things
and asking his uncle to help the boy. Joe put it in his shirt.

It was time to leave. The shopkeeper made food and gave it
to the boy for his trip. Joe opened his bag of dollars but Tony
said he wanted no payment. The boy insisted, saying that the
heavy silver would only slow him down. Finally, Tony took
half, agreeing to hold it until the Indian could return to the city
and claim it.

The boy went into the night and made his way across a
sleeping city. Near the lower end of the Hudson River water-
front, he found a boat tied at a wooden wharf. It had oars and
seemed to be small enough for one man to row. Joe stepped in,
and untied the rope. He reached into his pouch and stacked
three dollars on the dock. This should be ample payment, he
decided.

Joe rowed out into the current of a mighty river, where once
his ancestors had seen a strange, new ship from a different land.
The river was dirty and full of garbage; the Indian was
wounded and fleeing for his life.

9

A Wounded Fugitive

Joe Two Trees found his way to the far shore, and near dawn was on a beach. He pushed the rowboat back into the flow and let it drift away. It would not be found to betray his presence. A grove of trees stood above the high-tide line, and they would offer a temporary shelter. It was early spring again, and Joe felt a stirring inside when he noticed green buds and early-sprouting shoots. The Earth Mother was awakening, and she would look after her lost woodland child. He spent the day in the protective cover of the trees, and let sleep heal his body.

When he woke, it was almost dark. He felt much better than he had in the morning. Opening the small bundle given by Tony, the boy ate some food. Soon he felt like going on. Tony's hand-drawn map led him in a southerly direction, and he followed it through the night. The land was mostly woods, but here and there he passed farms with buildings and livestock sheds. He avoided these, knowing that New York City was not yet far behind. Perhaps these people had already been alerted to watch for an Indian boy. He walked on until the waking birds began to warn of dawn. Before the light was full, he found a thick growth of bushes near a small creek. Shelter, water, and the food in the bundle were all he needed. This would be the next encampment.

Seeing rabbits scurry away as he approached, Joe made a snare. Soon the flint knife was cleaning a fat cottontail. Joe made a tiny fire, rotating a stick between his palms into a softer

piece of wood, and fanning the resultant spark to life. Shortly, a
rabbit sizzled over the flames. That morning the boy had the
first hot meal he had consumed in nearly seven months. He ate
every scrap, and sucked each bone clean.

He slept again and later, when he woke, ate from the bundle.
This was a good place, thought Two Trees. The rabbits could
give food for a long time, and the water was at hand. He was
tempted to stay and live in this spot. The idea passed as he
reminded himself of Tony's uncle, and the farm. He took out
the letter and looked at its strange words. The boy wondered
how marks on paper could speak from one white man to another. He shrugged and decided this was one of many mysteries
in the world; mysteries he would never understand. The writing
of words that speak must be a privilege of only important people such as bosses and shopkeepers. He looked at the letter
until darkness made it futile. The words still said nothing, but
he would continue searching for the man to read them.

He wrapped his things in the bundle and cut a stick. Tying
the bundle to it, he balanced it on his healing shoulder and
started out. Animal eyes were all that watched him disappear
into the misty gloom. The night was young, the ground was
smooth, and Joe covered many miles before dawn brought the
next day.

As he walked, memories came and went. Long ago, his father had told him of this place. Although Eagle Feather had
never ventured this far, he had been told of the island. Joe's
grandfather, knowing that the Indian time was ending, had
tried to tell Eagle Feather as much of his heritage as possible.
The father had, in turn, told Two Trees. This had been, not so
long ago, the land of the Delawares. They had been called
Lenni Lenape, which meant "the real people." Joe wondered,
as he walked, whether they had been like the people of the
Turtle clan.

He judged that by now he had walked about the right distance. He would look for the uncle in the morning. A convenient brush patch served as sleeping quarters for the short time
left until dawn. In that cloudy awareness, when one is not yet
asleep, but not still awake, Joe saw Indian boys coming toward
him. He thought he heard them say "brother." But then he
slept and the vision was gone.

When morning came he found a clear brook and bathed. The road dust had accumulated on his clothing, and he scrubbed these out against a flat rock. He spread the clothes on some bushes to let a spring sun and breeze dry them. It wasn't long before he was dressed again. Hoping he looked fairly presentable, Joe set out to find the farm.

Beyond a grove of sassafras trees, smoke rose in a thin wisp. It must be a farmer's hearth fire. He walked through the trees and saw a farmyard. Pigs and chickens wandered about and there was a man near the far fence. Joe decided to ask this man about the farm he was seeking. Surely, he thought, one farmer would know another. He left the woody cover and walked confidently toward the man. As he approached, the man saw him and casually reached for a shotgun, which had been resting against the split-rail fence. He didn't point it or even raise it, so Joe continued toward him. When he was close enough, the boy spoke a greeting. The man returned his greeting with a smile. The smile made Joe feel better. He had not been comfortable about the gun. Now he saw that the man was neither angry nor fearful. He was only being cautious. Joe could well understand this.

Explaining his mission, Joe brought out the letter. The man said he had never heard the name Joe mentioned. He had been here only a short time though, having come from New York City himself. He told Joe that he had not liked life in the city. The boy quickly agreed. It was partly in order to give a reason for his leaving, but mostly it was simple truth. The farmer looked at Joe's letter and shrugged. The foreign words meant nothing to him.

I saw that Joe seemed weaker again, and asked if he wanted to finish telling me his story another time. He rested a bit, sipped at the Indian tea, and said he would continue. I could sense that the telling was important to him. I listened.

The farmer soon put aside his shotgun and seemed pleased to chat with the Indian boy. He said there was some work to be done. He would be glad to have his wife prepare a breakfast in return, if Joe would help him for a while.

They chopped firewood, split fence rails, and dug a garbage

pit together. The man worked shoulder to shoulder with the young Indian. When they finished, the sun was already quite high in the morning sky. The man wiped perspiration from his face as he looked up, then joked that a late breakfast was better than none at all, and they walked toward the house.

When the door opened, the farmer's wife showed momentary surprise, but it quickly faded into a smile. Joe realized that her surprise had been over the appearance of two people on the porch, where she had expected only her husband. The fact that one had cinnamon skin had not caused it. These were better people on the farms, thought Joe. They saw a man, when one stood before them, not his exterior alone. These must still be children of the Great Spirit. He was very glad that this spot had been his stopping place. Perhaps the Earth Mother had directed his feet to this farm, this place of growing things.

The woman moved rapidly around the small kitchen and soon eggs sizzled with bacon, while biscuits added aroma. Platters were set on a rough-hewn board table. When all sat down, the farmer bowed his head and spoke thanks to the "Heavenly Father." Joe also gave thanks, thanks for a small good thing that pushed aside the darkness for him.

The meal was served and Joe was familiar with eggs. He had often been sent to the swamp places in search of duck eggs when he was small. The bacon was new to him, and he enjoyed its strong flavor. Rolls, dipped with bee's honey, made a fine taste in his mouth. Cups of hot coffee washed down one of the best meals he had ever eaten.

No time was allowed for sitting after breakfast; not on a farm. Sitting was done after supper, when all the day's work was finished. The farmer said this and asked if Joe would like to work for more meals. The boy enthusiastically agreed, and they left for the fields. They hoed and weeded, carried water to the furrows, did all sorts of jobs. The animals needed water and feed; they hauled the feed out of a barn, the water from a well. The work was hard but it was pleasant. Toward noon, the farmer's wife brought food in a basket. The two stopped for a time to sit under a tree and eat. Lunch done, they continued with the farm work. As afternoon shaded into evening, they went to a hillside pasture and led the cattle to their night quarters. When the light was gone, the day's chores ended. The two walked toward the porch again. They stopped in the yard to draw buckets of water from the well. Using this water, they washed away the dirt of a farm day. The two entered to the smell of roasting meat, potatoes, muffins, and all sorts of things not known to the boy. They both were tired, but they were very hungry.

Joe lay down that night in a barn with clean hay for his bed. The sweet smell of it was good, and he slept in more comfort than he had in months. The meal, and friendship, gave him a warm glow that lasted through night into morning. He woke happy and refreshed, ready for work. When the farmer came out on his porch, Joe stood, already washed and anxious to begin the day.

They led the livestock to pasture and returned for their morning meal. Having eaten, they began the farm day. Their hours passed quickly and too soon, it seemed, supper was done. Again, the boy lay in the fragrant hay. Before sleep came, he watched a spider weave its web. The little creature worked so precisely that Joe became fascinated by its motions. It first strung a silken thread from an overhead beam. Climbing back to the middle of this thread, it sat and waited for a breeze. When one came, it blew the insect across to a pitchfork handle that stood up from a bale of hay. There the spider attached its line and crept back to the center. Continuing this, it soon had a pattern of silk that looked like wagon wheel spokes. This part completed, it hopped from spoke to spoke, spinning cross-members in a circular pattern. Joe watched the spider calculate and measure as it went. Each circle was almost perfectly spaced from the one made before it. The spider finished, and sat quietly to wait for its supper. Soon, a small moth bumbled into the glistening, nearly invisible net. The spider raced in; supper was ready.

The boy watched as the spider ate, and he reflected. All creatures had a way to get their meals. Even the spider spun its trap each night, for that was the way it found food. Only I, thought the boy, have not found my way. Should I be Indian, should I load boxes, should I farm? Where would Joe finally find the right way for his life? These were the thoughts that occupied his mind as he dozed into sleep. When he woke, the spider had taken down its web and was gone. It had left to sleep in a hidden place until dusk called it out again. Joe envied it for the routine its life held.

The next morning, Joe rose, washed, and again joined in the farm work for his keep. He felt that this life would satisfy him, but he knew enough of farming to see that harvesttime would come soon. After the harvest, Joe knew from all his own experience, farm work would be slow and help would not be needed. The boy didn't need to be told that by September or October he would not be a help to this family, but a drain on it. He decided that this would also be the case with Tony's uncle. On that farm he would not even have helped with the summer work. He would be unwanted at best. The idea of haven that had occupied him during his trip from New York evaporated like morning fog. He would soon be alone again. He wasn't worried about food. He still had money and knew how to live off the land, if need be. His worry was a different thing. It was made up of winter, loneliness, and other concepts not fully formed, like clouds in his mind. He thought that it would be wonderful indeed to own a farm someday; and build a log house with a fireplace, where he could keep a dog, perhaps, for company. But his few silver dollars would never buy land. Even if he had enough money, he was a hunted criminal who could not settle in one place. He would have to move on.

Each day the sun set farther to the south, and Joe knew it would soon make the crooked walk of winter. He worked with the farmer through the waning days of autumn into Indian summer. One day, all was done. The crops were harvested; the fodder was ready for the animals. The farm season was ended. The small amounts of winter work could easily be handled by one man.

That night, the young boy gathered a few belongings into his rag bundle. In the hayloft he prepared a spot for sleeping, and, curling up there, began to cry. At some time during the darkness, he fell asleep. Morning came, and he ate with the family. He told them he would move on now, and they agreed. The boy thanked them for their food and kindness.

10

The Hardest Winter

The road had a familiar feel to his feet. As he walked, Joe reflected that the road, any road, had become an old friend to him. Whether woodland trail, dirt or cobbles, the road always led to another place, a new start. He thought about his condition and, surprisingly, was pleased. He knew that he had eaten well, was healthy and strong, and still had heavy silver bouncing against his thigh. Girded with these as armor, he went forth to face winter and the white man's world.

He walked until the waters of Arthur Kill stopped him, then followed the shoreline until reaching a spot that must have been near the present Outerbridge Crossing. There, Two Trees saw a man sitting in a partly hidden rowboat. His gun suggested duck hunting, but all that Joe saw told him no ducks would come to the spot. He waved, and the hunter waved back, motioning him over. As Joe approached, the man said something about not worrying about scaring the ducks. He hadn't seen any. The boy looked up at the clouds overhead and noted the wind direction. He squinted at the New Jersey shore and saw a small cove with tall bulrushes around it. He knew, by an instinct deep in his being, that no duck would fly under such low clouds to sit near a windward shore. He remembered the lessons his father had taught him at Turtle Cove and Vagabond Bay.

Two Trees, the Indian, pointed out these things to the hunter. They were a part of his heritage. It was bits of knowledge such as these which had provided food for his people, long before any man had hunted with a gun on this continent. He visualized the fall hunts at Turtle Cove, near his old home that his father had told him about. The men would hide in the tall reeds, reeds like those across the water. In this cove, he thought, would be ducks, feeding and gathering together.

Joe offered to do the rowing if the man would come across to look for the seabirds. He told the hunter that he needed a way to cross anyhow, and would pay him for the use of the rowboat. The hunter, still a bit skeptical, finally agreed.

Two Trees pushed the small boat off a sod bank and into the main flow. The wind kept trying to force the two back into the frothy surf. Once he got the feel of the oars though, the boat moved off into the wind. Soon, the boy had established a rhythm, and the boat moved well. At each stroke, the bow would push into the whipped waves and throw up a fine mist of cold water. Joe felt, and took note of, the chilly bite in the early winter wind. Soon, he knew, would come a "tracking snow." This was what his father had always called the first white powder of winter. This was the snow that showed footprints of animals that had eluded him all summer. When the tracking snow came, he could follow them right to their lairs.

Joe directed the boat toward the left side of the cove he had spotted. Soon the boat was near enough to see into the protected water. Ducks were there. Scaup, black ducks, canvasbacks, and many others were rafted near the head of the tiny bay. The hunter was pleased and amazed. This young boy had been able to point to the spot from the other shore, and he had been right!

Joe rowed the boat onto a bank and pulled it up a short way. The hunter pulled off his leather boots and rolled up his trousers. The two waded and crawled to a spot on the edge of the bulrushes. The sound of gunfire shook the reeds. The hunter had time to fire and reload several times while the ducks, unaware of the men, and only frightened by the noise, still milled around the cove. With each salvo, more ducks dropped to the water's surface. When the last birds had flown off, ten remained to be collected. The two men took their boat and rowed into the cove. Gathering the birds, they set out for a clear landing and came ashore on a pebble beach with trees just beyond. Joe offered money to the man for his passage, but it was refused. He told Joe that God had not put the water there to make him a rich man, but had quite possibly sent Joe to teach him about duck hunting. The two laughed together, comrades of the hunt. Joe was pleased at the mention of God. These people of the woodlands were still close to the Great Spirit, he thought.

Joe gathered sticks of wood and, twirling a pointed twig into dry pulp, had a fire crackling in minutes. The exhilaration of the hunt, combined with the clean tang of autumn air, had produced fine appetites. Two fat ducks turning on green wood spits became meals of both quantity and quality. It was good to sit once more by a campfire. The young Indian felt his thoughts move through the mists of many seasons, back to other fires, other places. It was comfortable to let the warmth of the embers and the conversation bring back old, buried feelings. Joe pushed back the comfort and warmth by reminding himself consciously that this was now, not then. Many problems confronted him for which he had only vague, half-formed solutions. He was partly aware that some of these problems were such that he had not even conceived of them as yet. Better, he thought, frankly to ask this man, who was still partially in his debt, than leave and lose the small chance for advice.

Joe told the hunter a bit of his story, carefully avoiding any reference to his use of the flint knife in self-defense. He asked how he could make a place in this new white world.

The man thought for a time and finally suggested that Joe might find small, odd jobs at the many farms that stretched across the state of New Jersey. Farmers would probably offer food in return for woodchopping and other work. In this manner Joe could work his way across the state into the Pennsylvania country where, it was said, new coal fields were opening. These mines would certainly need all the workers they could get. Joe knew very little of coal. He remembered that some stores in the city had burned it for heat, and it was black. The hunter explained it was dug from deep underground and only a strong back was required. Having that prerequisite, Joe decided to go to Pennsylvania and try mining coal.

It was late now, and the man said he must be going home. Joe was sorry to see him leave. He watched as the wind pushed the small boat back toward Staten Island. This seemed as good a place to spend the night as any other, so Joe gathered reeds and pine boughs for bed and shelter. Soon he was lying in a lean-to, peering into the depths of a tiny fire. The wind whistled overhead, but he was as comfortable as he needed to be. In the mellow firelight, he reflected on his experience with the strange white men. Some had been bad, some had been kind, others indifferent to him. He thought it strange, though, that none had hated him as his father had said they did in the old time. He recollected the workers' laughter as they said "Indian Joe, Indian Joe." The laughs had been cheerful, not malicious, as if directed at a foe. Gradually, he saw the reason. He was no longer the enemy, as his people had been perceived in the old time. He was only an oddity, a freakish being from another time.

Morning came, still and bright. During the hours after midnight, a light sprinkle of snow had changed the hard contours of rocks and trees into softly rounded curves. The wind died before sunrise, and now the world glittered with cold majesty. The snow, thought Two Trees, was a garment of great beauty sent to the Earth Mother by Tchi-Manitou. It must have been a robe of light such as this that she had worn during her descent from the floating Island in the story of The Beginning. But such thinking could not help a would-be coal miner. Now it was time to move on. If he couldn't find his way to this Pennsylvania before frigid north winds locked the earth in its frozen chains, he'd better have a suitable place to lay up until spring.

Joe packed his things and set off from farm to farm, as the hunter had advised. Here he dug or there he chopped. He was allowed the use of wells and haylofts along his way, but soon saw that he could provide better for himself than the meager rations offered in return for a day of hard labor. One morning, he crossed a narrow, icebound stream. A thick grove of pines stood on the northern bank. Those trees would break the cold wind. No farms were nearby. Cattails and bulrushes grew where a beaver dam had created a small pond. By dusting snow from the ice, Joe saw through to the stream bottom. He noticed several dark shapes facing into the current, undulating slowly back and forth. Trout! This would be the winter place. Roots, fish, and rabbits from the brush along the banks would serve well until warmth brought back berries and fruit.

Branches were bent to form a round-topped framework. The frame was thatched with reeds and bark. The chinks were plugged with mud and clumps of uprooted grass. Inside, the floor was covered with hastily woven reed mats. Soon, a fire sent plumes of thin smoke to the center hole in the roof. The wigwam was ready.

A short walk upstream disclosed many rabbit runs trod into the dry grass and undergrowth. Branches were soon cut with the flint knife, and a line of snares set. The rabbit fur would not serve as well as bearskin, but patched into a blanket, it would keep one warm on a cold night. The flesh would not be venison, but it would still fill a hungry belly. Surveying his work, the Indian nodded, satisfied that all was done well. He set out and walked in a mile wide circle.

Exploring the land served many needs. By the time Joe returned to the new wigwam he knew where he could hide nearby, should danger threaten. The lack of boot prints in mud or snow reassured him that no white man lived near this place. The marks of animals told which species lived here and in what numbers. The place had a good feel to it. He entered the hut and poked the coals back to life. This night's fare was only roots, but the snares, he knew, would soon improve his diet.

Two Trees set several deadfalls around his hut. These were logs, balanced against nearby trees and set with trip lines. They would announce any visitors. This done, he retired to the warm hut. Joe felt something near pleasure as he sat before the tiny flames. Shadows danced across the floor and walls, and he had a sensation of being in the company of his own kind. Closing his eyes, he imagined hearing the deep snore of his father's breathing, and the gentle sigh of his mother. He knew these sounds to be only wisps of the mind, but they pleased him. It was a long time before he could force his eyes open again. When he did, a subtle difference in the wind sound attracted his attention. He noted that the wind had turned, and now blew from the northeast. Joe opened the flap door and stood up in dark shadows to gather more weather signs. The moon still shone as it had earlier, but the half-orb cast a different light now. It was pale, almost sickly. Around the pale body shone a circular halo. The maple branches that Two Trees cut that day had poured out sap, and it was now frozen into long icicles.

Fingers of grayish cloud were climbing up from the east, obscuring the stars. The Indian knew that snow was coming. This was not to be a tracking snow, but the kind that comes on strong wind, to pile high and keep one in his wigwam. This was not the time for sleep. He cut branches and reinforced the windward side of the hut. The wind-to-be could easily rip away the thatching before a protective layer of snow covered it. When he was satisfied that the wall would hold up, he thought about his rabbit snares. Better to check them now, by moonlight, thought Joe, than lose them in the coming snow. Checking each he retrieved two rabbits. These were already frozen stiff. He tripped the other snares so no rabbit might be trapped and not found to be used for food and blanket. Then Two Trees took a last look around and, satisfied that he had done his best, entered the hut. He could sense something in the air. Any modern weatherman would have said the barometer was falling rapidly, but Joe knew only that the air felt wrong.

Within one hundred feet of the young Indian, others were also dimly aware of the change. A great snowy owl had come down to New Jersey to escape the arctic winter. It perched above the wigwam, high in a pine tree, and nervously awaited the storm. A tiny kangaroo mouse, affected by the dropping air pressure deep in its subterranean nest, stretched his long hind legs in dreamless sleep. The beaver, icebound within his wooden lodge, gnawed thoughtfully at a bark-covered twig. Rabbits huddled together, gathering warmth from the many bodies in their underground labyrinth. Near the owl, a gray squirrel had rolled himself into a ball in his nest, tail acting as a blanket. The seeds and nuts inside his home of tight woven twigs and leaves would make trips to the ground unnecessary for the time being, but if the nest was blown down, it could be a sad event for any squirrel. Joe thought of his father's name for this animal. It had been hannick. He was cheered by the sudden memory.

All of nature was waiting for some event that none had experienced before. Each felt the impending menace, and knew it would be bad. Most of the woodland creatures had lived only a year, two, or three at most. Even the boy, in his short life, had not yet known a blizzard.

Joe checked the inside walls of his shelter and plugged small drafts with grass. He wrapped himself in reed mats and placed a small log on his fire. Having done all within his power, he left the outcome to his God. By midnight the wind had risen to a steady wail. It increased during the early hours of the morning and by dawn a fine snow was being pushed before it. Through the day, the wind-whipped snow became so heavy that visibility outside the hut was all but nonexistent. Toward midday, Two Trees went out to gather more wood. He saw that the storm might keep him imprisoned for a time. Wood meant fire and warmth. He had to push snow away from the entrance flap. It had already drifted to a depth of two feet. When he finally was able to squeeze through, his senses were assailed by an experience he had not had before. The wind raged and pulled at his clothes. The air was so cold that it hurt his chest when he inhaled. The driven snowflakes struck his bare hands and face with such force that each felt like a tiny needle driven into the flesh. His first impulse was to retreat back into the temporary sanctuary of the hut, but years of forest life forced his reason to prevail. With no fire, the hut would soon offer only the prospect of a cold, lingering death. He pushed through drifts and pulled at each exposed branch or twig. Joe cursed his carelessness. The extra wood should have been gathered before the storm had reached its full fury. Instead of trapping rabbits, he should have gathered the fuel to make warmth and light. Hunger could be endured for many days, but cold was an insidious killer. It could creep into the hut by night and invade the sleeping body. Without fur blankets to hold the body heat, Joe knew that fire was more than a luxury now. He gathered what wood he could, but the cold soon forced him back to shelter. During the remainder of the short afternoon, he made several forays and every twig still visible went into the hut. On his final trip, he explored the area under the thick roof of interlaced pine trees. Here, bare spots still existed on the otherwise covered ground. Joe pulled up tufts of dead grass and weeds. These, he forced into his jacket, trousers, and boots. The dry materials would add some small insulating quality to his clothing. Two Trees knew that he had now done all possible with the limited resources available. It was time to go back to the wigwam and wait.

Joe saw that the snow had already reburied his entrance, and he was forced to dig his way to the flap with bare hands. He noted that snow had drifted over the wigwam, and it now appeared as a small hill. Only the tiny chimney hole, with its blackened, sooty ring showed evidence that this mound was not a rock or beaver lodge. At least the snow would keep out wind. He entered.

Two Trees took one of his rabbits and skinned it. He cut the meat into pieces and placed them on a small ledge of snow where wind had forced through a crevice in the wall. The crevice was now frozen closed, but it provided a handy spot for cold storage. He did the same with the other rabbit. Joe looked at the few small scraps, and wondered. So little was the food made from two plump rabbits. How long would it last? How long would it need to last?

He sat by the fire and listened to the storm. The sounds were muffled now by the layer of snow over his hut, but the intensity seemed as great as it had earlier. The blizzard showed little sign of abating. It had blown for a night and a day. Joe was not happy at the prospect of still another night. He wondered if his hastily built hut would withstand the weight of drifted snow above. Unable to do anything further for his protection, he decided that food would help make sleep easier. Soon, two chunks of rabbit sizzled pleasantly over the small fire. The smell of roasting meat was a happy one. It helped raise the spirits of a very frightened young Indian. At some point during the cooking, he noticed that the smell had become stronger. Smoke was burning his eyes. Joe looked up and saw smoke billowed under the roof. The chimney hole had been snowed over. He took a long stick and poked the hole clear. This was to become necessary several more times during the long night. But the meat was done now, and Joe ate. The food warmed his insides as the fire did his wigwam, and soon he was cheered by happy thoughts. If the snow stopped soon, there were still ways to find food in the white world. He would make snowshoes of evergreen branches, bent and tied with bark. He would set snares for any animal that might venture out of its hiding place. He could even eat the tiny tree buds, bringers of spring leaves. If the hut held up, he knew he could still find sustenance on the blanketed land. Several times that night the shifting weight caused Joe's framework of saplings to bend or creak; but the green branches, though frozen, were resilient. Some cracked with a sharp sound, but the shelter held.

It was morning. Even in the dark of the snow-shrouded hut, he knew it was morning. His body told him, his senses all said morning, but there was no light. He had fallen asleep and now woke with a start. At first he was confused. The cold was no longer waiting to enter his body. It had. His hands and face were numb, his body and feet ached. The fire had gone out! Darkness was absolute, unrelieved by the smallest glimmer of light. Joe knew that some light would always penetrate into any snow he had ever known. This was deep snow. He knew he had been buried alive. All around, the snow had reached a height above the waist of a tall man, but Joe's hut was in a spot where it had drifted much higher. He tried to push a stick up through the smoke hole, but his reach was not enough to penetrate the thick mantle. Lashing two sticks together, he tried, and failed again. Lighting the fire was out of the question. Smoke would gather, filling the hut. It would quickly choke him.

Now was a time for both action and thought. Action came first. He was almost frozen stiff. Joe jumped and rolled. He beat at his arms and body. He twisted and ran in place. After a while, he could feel the cold being pushed out by exertion. The sluggish blood began to push through cold veins and reach nearly frozen extremities. Joe was far from warm, but he began to believe he might still survive. Once he was able to use his hands again, he methodically poked his stick through parts of the surrounding walls. He hoped to find a place where the wind had left only thin snow covering the hut. At last, he admitted to himself that there was no such place. The only way out of the trap was the way he had come in—through the entrance. Joe pulled the flap aside and began scooping out a low vestibule. He pushed the snow back toward the rear of his hut. His hands were very cold, but this was his only hope of escape. Thinking of the pouch, which still held his few silver dollars, Joe found it in the dark and used it over one hand as a mitten. The dollars that he spilled out might be lost in the snow, but that didn't seem very important. The hole grew, and finally, he could kneel in a crouch in front of the buried wigwam. By forcing his head and torso upward and then forward, he formed a rough step ahead of him. He dragged more snow down and back into the hut. It became a routine; dig, push body, dig, push again. The cold was biting and cruel. By now snow had found its way into his boots and down his neck. It melted slowly, sending trickles of ice water down his ribs and between his toes. But Joe had been toughened by a stern father in his early years. Eagle Feather had insisted on winter dippings at the icy creek near Mishow even when Two Trees was still more baby than boy. It will harden him, he had told a worried wife, and so it had. Joe could almost feel the presence of Eagle Feather offering encouragement, urging him on. At one point Joe felt something in the snow ahead, and his fogged mind, near hysteria, thought it to be the hand of Eagle Feather, come to pull him up. It was only the branching limb of a bush that he now recalled was about ten feet away from the hut. He pushed upward and noticed that the interwoven branches had kept snow from packing heavily. Using the branches as foot- and handholds, he forced his way upward. A diffused glow above told Joe that he was near the surface. After what seemed a long time, he was able to push an arm through, opening a small aperture. His eyes hurt at the sudden brightness. His ears picked up the twittering chatter of chickadees high in the pines. Tough little birds that they were, they too had survived the storm. Now they whistled greetings to the newly risen sun. The sound told Joe that the snow had passed. The boy pushed himself through the remaining snow, and emerged into a far different world than he had ever seen. Earth had lost her character. Only two colors remained; the blue of the cloudless sky against the endless white of snow. No shape remained to catch the eye, only the smooth, rounded contours of drifted snow. Where trees poked up through the white, they too were covered like pointed tents. Even the boughs of pine were covered and pulled almost flat against the trunks. Joe looked around for the great owl. It appeared to have left. Probably, it had gone farther south as soon as the storm allowed flight. The bird knew that game would be very scarce in this wasteland for some time to come; so did Joe.

Two Trees spent the next several hours improving the entrance. When he was able to pass from the hut below into the open air with relative ease, he cleared the snow from inside and opened his smoke hole again. With a small fire burning, the shelter was soon warm enough to allow him to remove and dry his clothes and boots. When the boots came off, Joe saw something he didn't like. Several toes were bluish-black. They felt numb, without sensation.

At this point in his story, Joe stopped and removed his boots. The very old man had trouble bending, but he managed to show me that several toes were now gone. I had never noticed this during our trips and adventures, but I saw it clearly that day. I wondered how the amputations of frost-dead toes had been accomplished without aid of a doctor, but didn't ask. I was afraid that I might already know. A flint knife could serve many needs.

The old man was visibly weaker, and he asked for water. I gave it to him and held the cup as he drank. I begged him to rest, but he could not. The story, he said, would not be finished if he took time for rest. If he could not tell the story, his spirit would be doomed to walk some shadow place, between the floating island and this world. He seemed to need the telling so badly that I had no choice but to listen. I think it was at this point I became aware that my friend, the last Bronx Indian, Joe Two Trees, was dying.

He continued the tale, telling of drying his clothes, and then looking over the surrounding area. The barren snowscape offered little that could be used toward survival. He had lived this long though, he would continue. Walking was impossible. Each attempted step plunged him in up to his armpits. He broke several pine branches loose and bent them into needle-webbed snowshoes. This done, he was at least able to move around the camp area. He had escaped from his living burial, but he was still trapped. While the prison had been enlarged, the bars were still as strong. He could only manage to move a few yards in any direction. Joe wished fervently that he had found this place earlier in the winter and put up food against such a catastrophe. The remains of one rabbit were his only provisions. By rationing, this might last a week. In that time other sustenance must be found.

Three days passed but the bitter cold would not allow the snow to melt. Some settling occurred, though, and movement around the wigwam became a bit easier. On the morning of the fourth day, Joe extended his search area. The need for food had become acute. The Indian crept to the top of a small hillock about a hundred yards away from his wigwam and peered over cautiously. He spotted motion. The tips of the branches of a small apple tree had protruded through the snow, and a rabbit was gnawing at the bark and buds. Joe crawled toward the animal, not knowing how he would catch it, but knowing he must. As he approached, Joe was surprised that the furry, little creature didn't run off. Finally, the rabbit became aware of man-scent, and tried to flee, but days without food had weakened it. This wasn't a rabbit from the underground warren. This one had been trapped above by the storm. Half frozen and nearly starved, it was unable to escape from the youth. Joe simply crawled over and picked it up. The rabbit, a young female, protested with a few weak kicks, but soon stopped. Joe held her for a moment and then placed her inside his jacket. The rabbit sat quite still, afraid, but warm for the first time in many days.

Joe walked back to the shelter with a meal secure inside his coat. The Great Spirit had provided for him. Once in the hut, he took the furry bundle from against his chest and placed it on the floor. The young hare sat and watched for a long time. She was too weak to flee. There was nowhere to go if she could. It was warm and dark here, almost like the burrow she had lost during the blizzard. Joe watched. He saw that the animal was afraid. He began to wonder whether Tchi-Manitou had led Joe to the rabbit for food or the rabbit to Joe for shelter. He took a green branch from his pile of firewood and held the bud-end twigs out. The animal accepted and soon was happily nibbling. There would be no roast meat tonight. Joe reasoned that other means still remained to be explored. There were the buds to eat. In the morning he would try to capture a trout from the buried brook. He would not kill one who had survived the storm. He would not kill the creature sent by his Father for him to protect.

Joe broke off more twigs for the animal and returned to the surface. He walked all the way across the grove of pines, following the tracks of hannick, the gray squirrel. Hannick had not stayed in his safe nest after all. The trail ended abruptly, and the snow told a story, several days old, of the squirrel's last meal before departing. Two small, red stains and a few hairs were framed between the imprints of huge wings stretching four feet from tip to tip. The owl would live to find a mate and rear her young when spring came. The simple equation had been fulfilled. Some must die for others to live. It was the great plan. Even as he thought this, Joe worked to gather twigs for his rabbit.

Suddenly, a thought came. Hannick, the squirrel was dead! Joe ran, slipping and falling, to the wigwam. He took off his clumsy snow shoes and looked up at the squirrel's leaf nest. Jumping, he grabbed the lowest branch and pulled himself up. Climbing was easy. Each branch offered a hold along the way to the empty nest. He soon reached it and pulled it loose. Its careless owner wouldn't need it again. Joe dropped it to the snow and slid down the trunk. He picked up the prize and ran to his hut. The small treasures within included seeds, nuts, and acorns, all edible to some degree. Here was at least one meal. The twigs added to the firewood pile. The leaves and soft grass from inside the nest helped Joe's bed become a little warmer.

Later, he decided to try for the fish that wintered under ice on the stream bottom. Joe cleared the snow from over the place where he had seen them days earlier. With a small rock, taken from the fire pit, he chipped out a hole in the thick ice. When the hole was wide enough, he looked in, but the noise of chopping had scared the fish off. Two Trees covered the hole with a pine bough to keep it from freezing again and left to make a spear. Hickory would be good wood for the spear, but none was available, so Joe cut a long, thin shoot from the apple bush. He trimmed the end to a point and undercut it to form a barb. Taking the green wood to his hut, Joe placed the tip into fire and rotated it slowly. Satisfied that the flames had hardened it enough, he went to the ice hole. By lying on the ice, he was able to peer under one corner of the pine-needled covering and see into the little world below. Winter had come here also. No minnows darted back and forth. No crayfish crept among the pebbles. No insects were to be seen. The stream was asleep. All its tiny residents had retreated into the muddy banks, or slept, sheltered under bottom stones. Only the little fishes with spots and a band of color along each side were not gone. Unlike the turtles, frogs, and other stream dwellers, the trout passed his winter without sleeping. He found his place in a deep water spot, and rested. Joe could see that several had returned, having forgotten the noise. They were back now, as he had seen them before, slowly finning in the icy current. By inching his spear into the clear water, he was able to slowly bring it near a fish. A sudden thrust and the fish was impaled. Joe carefully withdrew the shiny creature and placed him in snow, away from the hole. He took no chance that his meal might flip its way back into the stream. Before the daylight had begun to fail, three fish were captured. They lay, side by side, frozen hard as wood.

The smoke that came from Joe's hut that night had a pleasant aroma. He slept with the warmth of food within him. Late in the flickering darkness of low flames, the rabbit nestled against Joe's leg. He awoke and saw, but did not move. He smiled and went back to sleep.

That winter was long, and very hard. Joe's toes ached and bled much of the time, but gradually they healed. There was no early thaw that year, and snow covered the land all through the months of long nights. Joe often lost track of the progress toward spring. He would look, on a clear night, to the stars, but they still held their winter positions in the frosty sky. Once, he saw the aurora borealis stretched across the northern horizon, like a sweeping curtain of light. It was first white, then blue, yellow, green, and red. Joe wondered if it might be a message from his father, but unable to decipher it, he simply enjoyed its beauty.

The days and weeks were long. Sometimes the young man wondered if the spring would come at all. Sometimes he would begin to despair. Often he felt warm tears welling in his eyes, but he would force them away. He saw himself as a man now, and knew that Eagle Feather would not have approved of tears from his man-son. Then he would play with the rabbit. The cheery little animal was good to have. Joe talked to it and held it, and the gathering of food for it gave him something to think of beyond his own needs.

Then one day, he noticed something strange. The fear beast that had haunted him during his first winter alone, the winter after he buried his mother, had not come. The horrible loneliness that threatened to destroy all other thoughts was gone. He knew he had felt fear this winter, but it was a good fear. It was the kind that warned one, and helped one to be more careful.

Fear of hunger, cold, and even of death, were kinds of fear that could be understood. They were not the sick fear of loneliness that lived in the shadows and beyond the flap of the wigwam. Joe wondered if the beast still lived somewhere inside him, or at his old home place, or if he had beaten it. He hoped he had, for more than anything, he dreaded its return.

But the beast did not return that winter. The trout became more scarce as time passed. The meals were sometimes very meager. Joe grew thin. Nothing lasts forever, though, and even that winter finally began to die. Warm days came and melted off some snow cover. With the newly uncovered resources, Joe ate better, as did his rabbit. Cold north winds still blew, but the time between the warm days grew shorter and shorter. Spring was coming.

Soon, the snow was gone and the creek ice began to break and float downstream. The great plan had made one more full circle. Joe felt foolish now, as he thought back to his doubts during the bleak days of January and February. The great plan would continue, he now knew, even when he was gone. New trout came downstream to replace those Joe had caught. Green shoots appeared along the banks. The rabbit began to spend much time grazing outside the shelter. She wandered a little farther each day. At last, she didn't return. Joe was worried, and he walked the area searching for her. He couldn't find her and finally returned to his hut. Joe hoped that she had simply gone back to her own kin, and not been found by a hawk or owl. The next day, at sundown, she was back. She stayed the night but left early the following morning. As the warming days passed, she came less often. Joe began to place her food outside the hut. Sometimes it would be gone and sometimes not. He would find her accidentally on his daily forays. Occasionally she would allow him to come up and pet her. Usually she shied off. Joe saw that the closeness of two winter comrades was wearing away. He wasn't surprised. It was spring and she wanted her own. She had that right. Then came a time when Joe thought he had lost her forever. He hoped to see her one more time, but the food he put out each evening now stood untouched in the morning. The rabbit was gone, returned to the wild. Joe felt happiness at the thought that she was with her kind, but it was a happiness touched by sorrow.

The sorrow passed in the warm weather of April. Joe's days were spent in hunting and fishing, gathering and picking. He was weak from long months of confinement and poor diet. He knew that he must strengthen his body with food and rest. When he had done this, he would go on to the coal country. The late spring and early summer brought such bounty to the New Jersey creek land that Joe was tempted to begin storing for winter. He could stay here and live well. Next spring would be time enough for mining coal. The thought gradually died. Joe was still sure he wanted a place in the white man's society. He gazed off toward a setting sun and wondered what awaited him in Pennsylvania.

That night, Joe ate a hearty meal. He could feel that strength had returned to his young body. The foods of summer had put flesh back on his gaunt frame. It was time to leave this place. Even as he thought this, he was sure he would always remember it. There had been the rabbit. There had been the fighting for life and winning.

He took dried foods and prepared them for his trip. Later he put his belongings in a rag and tied them to a stick. He left the small bundle near the flap, where he could pick it up as he left at first light. Sleep came quickly.

When the first rays of a yet unrisen sun had just begun to color the morning mists to rose, Joe was already awake. He lay for a few minutes, to savor the smells and sounds of the newborn day. A bird chirped, and he could picture it stretching small wings, unused for many hours. From far off, the odor of a skunk was carried on the damp air. Some fox had probably learned a hard lesson in the night. Above, a small brown owl hooted its forlorn goodbye to darkness. A splash gave evidence of trout feeding on hatching insects. The day had come.

Joe rose and took his bundle. He opened the flap and stood up in the half light. He looked down and stopped. There were tiny shapes all around his feet, and one larger one. In the dew-wet grass in front of the hut, many small rabbits nibbled, watched over by his winter friend. She had been gone for a purpose, thought the man. Joe reached down, but the furry young scattered. He motioned to the mother, however, and she approached. Hesitantly at first, then more confidently, she came to the hand that had touched her many times before. Two

Trees knelt in the damp grass for several minutes caressing his former pet. Then the new mother gathered her children and brought them to a brush pile. When they were safely inside, she turned and watched the Indian. He had also turned, toward the west. As he walked, Joe Two Trees looked back and saw the rabbit. He continued on his way again and thought that even though he had saved her from the storm and fed her all winter, it was she that had given the greater gift.

11

The Cave Bear

There was a warm happiness inside as he walked along. The rising sun soon warmed his back as well. But the happiness was to be short-lived. After several hours, Joe neared a small farmhouse. He decided to stop and ask directions. He knew Pennsylvania was west, but had no idea of how far. A man opened the door to Joe's knock, but quickly started to close it again. Through the small crack left open, he yelled that he wanted no escaped slaves on his land. Then the door slammed shut.

Joe was very confused. He didn't know that word, "slave." He didn't know that the farmer, who in all probability had never seen an Indian, must have mistaken Joe's dark features for those of a black man. Joe walked thoughtfully that day, wondering why the man had called him "slave"—"escaped slave."[1]

As he continued west, Joe received mixed receptions at the farms he encountered. Some of the farmers, or their wives, were cool, some civil, but at least he was not mistaken for a slave again. Occasionally, he did work in return for food. He pushed on and one day someone told him that he was in Pennsylvania. The words excited him. Joe asked where he could find the coalfields. The stranger seemed surprised. Coal country was far to the north, he said, near Scranton and Wilkes-Barre. Coal coun-

[1] This was about 1857. The Underground Railway was handling hundreds of escaping slaves; the country was polarizing into North and South.

try was far indeed. He had no way of knowing how far, but he thought another winter living as an Indian would not be the worst thing that could happen, and he could start out for the mines in the spring. He started north, but this time he would find the winter place early enough to collect food and stores. This time he would use the Indian summer as the Maker had intended it. He would prepare. Unlike the previous year, he would be ready for winter when it came.

After September had grudgingly moved aside, replaced by October, Joe began to look for a place. Each day he moved north, but more slowly now. He was evaluating the land as he passed. Was there water that would still be accessible when the ice came? Were there stands of pine to break the north wind's sweep? Game? Fish? Were there all the things that, woven together, would form the fabric of survival? He kept going north, looking for the place he would know as home for at least half a year. Finally, he found it. The spot had come to exist thousands of years before, when a meandering river formed an oxbow bend on its western flank. The eastern side had eroded a steep cliff in reddish sandstone. Over the centuries trickling water had eaten away a cave in the base of the cliff. This would be ideal. The cave would be a protected spot. The walls of stone offered a security that could not be found in any wigwam. Joe looked at the thick, swampy growth in the river bottomland. The ancient oxbow had filled in and was full of reedy bushes. Game would be plentiful there, thought Joe. Edible roots and useful trees were all about. Here would be the winter place. Joe smiled.

It was still early in the afternoon, and Joe decided to explore within the new home. He walked in and soon realized the cave was deeper than he had thought. He rounded a slight bend, and the light began to fade. He could still see, though, and continued. Suddenly a dark form blocked his way and there was an angry deafening roar. The pain came so unexpectedly that Joe wasn't sure he had been knocked down until he was on his feet again. The form stood over him and howled in fierce, echoing indignation. In the dim light, Joe could see that a large bear had also wanted this cave for winter. The Indian turned and ran toward the daylight. The bear, seeing that he had won, did not follow.

Back in the warm sunshine, Joe looked behind and saw that he was not being pursued. He sat and felt his chest. The great paw had bruised him, but no bones were broken. Had he been tensed and rigid, expecting danger, the blow might well have smashed him. But loose and relaxed, the energy had caused him to stumble backward, and roll with the impact. He sat for a time and thought. Should he move on? Should he give up the good winter spot? Or, should he challenge the great Konoh, as his people had done in the old time? Might he conquer the cave, and a fine winter blanket with it? The decision came quickly. Joe would stand, and fight for this place.

When night came, he slept among the reeds. Joe ate dried fruit and watched the stars for a time before sleep came. By the time his eyes slid shut, a plan had formed in his mind. The almost feral man had already met the great animal. He knew where it would be in the cave. The combat plan for the next day was drawn. Joe slept soundly. He awoke before dawn, sore but alert, ready to begin.

First he used his knife to cut a stout spear of hickory. He tapered the end to a gradual point. No barbs were formed along the tip. Joe reasoned that he might have a chance to withdraw the spear after the first strike, and stab again. Barbs would hinder this. Next, he cut another hickory staff and split its end. He inserted the flint blade of his knife and fastened it with bark. This spear would be for throwing. It might not be as effective as one jabbed by hand, but luck could make it find a vital spot. In any case, Joe knew it would draw blood. Then he gathered bunches of dry grass. He tied them into bundles and inserted several dry cattails into each. After he had about a dozen, he lit the first one.

Joe ran into the cave and dropped the burning bundle, almost between the bear's great frontpaws. He was gone before the animal could react. A howl of fright split the air as Joe raced out of the darkness. He waited a few minutes and delivered another smoking bundle, and later another. Soon, a trickle of smoke was oozing from the top of the entrance. Now and then a growl or snarl could be heard from inside. Joe continued with the burning grass until all the bundles were inside the cave, contributing to a general smudge. The interior was a thick haze of eye-biting, acrid smoke. Joe took up his two spears and positioned himself to one side of the cave mouth. He hefted the flint-tipped spear in his right hand. It had good weight. It would throw well. But Joe tried not to deceive himself. The actual killing, he was sure, would be done with the wooden spear, hand to claw. A shudder passed through the Indian, but it was not born of fear.

With a bellow, the bear burst blindly out of the cave. As soon as he had left the smoke behind, the beast roared and threw himself up onto his hind legs, challenging his tormentor. The sight of the giant carnivore, standing much taller than a man, was an awesome one. Joe hesitated, wondering if his sticks would prove a match for this monster. But the hesitation was only momentary, and before the bear had regained its sight, the flint had been thrown. It arced into the soft belly, thrusting into the vital organs. The bear clawed at the protruding spear and managed to pull the wooden shaft loose. The flint stayed deep inside. The creature howled, wounded, but not crippled. Then he looked to the side and saw the man. Dropping down to all fours again, he lowered his head and charged. Joe sidestepped the lumbering attack and jabbed the neck as it presented itself. Joe knew that he had little chance of defeating the animal if it continued to attack on four feet. His only hope was to goad it into rising back to its hind legs. In that way, it would again expose its vital areas to the spear. Several more times Joe poked at the beast, but the injuries inflicted, although bloody ones, were only minor. The bear, having been badly hurt once, was hesitant to expose his weak spot again.

Joe saw that the bear would eventually catch him if it continued these frontal charges. The outcome would be death to the Indian. He had to do something. He hadn't counted on the bear's stubbornness. He had to force it up, but how?

An idea flashed. It was chancy, and involved turning his back on the determined animal, a most dangerous act, but it might work. He turned and ran toward the cave. Inside, he grabbed up a still burning torch and turned back to the cave entrance. He reached it just as the bear did. Joe held the torch out and let the animal's momentum force it into his face. The bear screamed in pain as the flames reached its already sore eyes, and it rose to his hind legs. Joe fell to one knee and braced the spear on the stone beneath him. When the bear came down, body weight forced the spear through his chest and out between his shoulders. Howling fearfully, the badly wounded animal fell to the ground and thrashed wildly in every direction. Large clots of blood splashed across the cave walls and onto Joe's body. Two Trees picked up a big rock and bashed the bear's skull in with it. The skin would make a fine winter blanket indeed, and Joe could almost taste his coming supper of bear steak.

Joe used the weeks of Indian summer as the Great Spirit had intended. He made the cave into a warm, comfortable dwelling, and prepared for the cold time ahead. The surrounding countryside offered many kinds of food. Two Trees gathered and stored. As the days grew shorter, he worked with a dedication that only necessity can foster. By the time ice began to show on the river each morning, Joe was ready. The midday sun still melted it, but winter, he knew, was almost upon the land.

With food and supplies around him, Joe felt more secure than he had in two years. He had stretched the skin of Konoh on the ground and pegged it in place. He scraped all the flesh and fat away and rubbed it with oak leaves. The tannic acid cured the hide, but Joe never knew of the acid. These were simply the same leaves his father had used, and his grandfather, to prepare the skins of deer and other animals. The final result had been a blanket, or robe, that gave Joe a feeling of pride. In the chill of early morning, Joe often wore the skin. Frequently, he wore it even after the sun's warmth had made it unnecessary. There was a special feel for him in the robe made from the skin of Konoh, the great bear he had killed.

Often, Joe would crouch in the mouth of his conquered cave, looking out across the land. The gold and red colors of fall brought strong feelings to him. They were deep feelings, rooted not in the mind, but in some other part of his being. He would caress the thick fur and try to understand. It was almost like listening to someone talk from far away. The words were lost on the wind, but their emotion could still be felt. Joe knew part of it was the bear. He had never thought Tchi-Manitou would allow him the privilege of meeting such an animal; that was a part of the old time. The Maker had given bears then so that his people could prove their valor. Konoh had been a part of being Indian. Joe would pull the robe close around him, and feel that he had proved himself. But in the same instant, the question would arise. Who was there to know that he had proved himself, or care? Two Trees knew that the old time was gone forever, but in some different part of his mind he was drawn toward all the acts and deeds that would make him an initiated Algonquin brave.

The strange thoughts lasted, locked in struggle within him. Through the waning autumn, and into the weeks of snow, Joe found himself thinking in odd, mixed concepts. One day he saw himself as Joe, traveler in the American world, soon to work at mining coal. He felt that although this world had been a harsh experience so far, it was about to become good. He would find the place for Joe in it. Next day he was Two Trees, killer of Konoh, warrior blessed by Tchi-Manitou. He was Indian, given this land from the beginning by his Maker, owing explanation to Him alone.

The winter was long and Joe had much time to think. Perhaps the winter gave him too much time. The struggle in his mind continued, and he became very confused. He wanted this American life, but he needed the Indian way. As winter passed, Two Trees often thought of his old home. The place back at Hunter Island sometimes came in dreams so real that he was unsure, on waking, if he had ever left. Joe could see that he had killed not only the bear, but the fear beast as well. Maybe he should go back. He vacillated between the two ideas many times during the long, frozen nights.

Although the winter seemed much longer, spring finally came in its proper time. As his people had done for thousands of years before him, Joe gave fervent thanks to the Creator for giving all things new life. He walked over the greening hills each day and felt more a part of the woodlands with each circuit of the sun. His Indian spirit was renewed, given new life with each bursting bud and probing, green shoot. Joe saw, and realized, that he was more Indian now than even in the days of Eagle Feather. Back at Hunter Island he had been only boy. Now, proven in combat and ordeal, he was man.

That spring, the Indian, for that he was again, came very close to turning back. He thought he might spend one more season at the cave in this bountiful country and then retrace his path to the city. The bloody night of death would probably have been forgotten by then. He could visit with his friend Tony for a day and then return home. He could return to the home of his ancestors. It would be better, he reasoned, near their spirits than lost and alone in a strange place.

Two Trees procrastinated for several weeks. Sometimes he was sure return was best. But a small doubt held him back. The doubt was born of curiosity. Joe wondered what he might see if he continued on. What might he miss by turning back? The journey had already shown him things so strange that sometimes he thought awe and amazement were his traveling companions. There was the bear. Surely he never would have met Konoh in his old home. Perhaps the Maker had sent this great beast to reward Two Trees. Joe fingered the single tooth that he had saved. The large fang hung around his neck, a permanent reminder of manhood. If the bear had been a reward, then it was also a sign. It could be a sign for Joe to go on. Perhaps the Maker had some obscure reason for wanting this.

Still not entirely sure, one morning Joe packed his things. He rolled the skin and carried it over his shoulder. It was heavy and bulky, but leaving it behind was unthinkable. The great skin would be blanket or tent, lean-to or robe. It would also be many other things; things that had no names, things of the spirit and the heart.

12

The Coal Mine

Once again, Joe's feet felt the familiar friendship of the road. He walked north. He didn't look back as he left the cave and river valley. If he did, he knew, he might stay. Two Trees continued across the beautiful land. Occasionally he came to a town, but skirted around, not wanting to leave his woods. Now and then he would stop at some isolated farm and ask directions. He never asked for work now, however. Two Trees lived off the land and the provisions he carried. The wooded country was largely unsettled, and when night came, it was easy to find a good campsite. Joe hoped that the destination would be as good as the journey.

Sometimes he saw other people along the way, but he instinctively avoided them. As when he left Hunter Island, he shunned any contact with these white people. Joe often wondered why he did this. He now spoke their language passably. He had worked with them. He understood their motives to some degree. But only the need for directions sometimes forced him to seek them out. Two Trees would sit, in the early summer heat, to rest and think. He had met both good and bad among them. He certainly did not hate them. Some had even been kind to him. Why did he feel apart? Why, when he thought of it, was the white man always "them"?

The old man paused to rest and catch his breath. I asked if there was anything he wanted; anything I could do. He silently shook his head. The sun had moved to an open patch between the branches, and from where I sat, his head was silhouetted against the sharp glare of winter. All details were lost as bright light streamed past his face, and the effect has always stayed, almost photographically, in my memory. As he gazed motionless into the flames, I noted the profile of my friend. Burnished by the light as it was, it might have belonged to a young man or an old man, or it could have been carved in stone. It wasn't Oriental, or Caucasian. It wasn't Negroid. It was something I can only call "other." As the profile was presented to me that day, I noticed all the things about it that had escaped my eyes before. I began to have some inkling of what Joe was trying or struggling to make me understand. He hadn't known the words to say, but his message was one of cultural difference. He was trying to describe, in simple terms, how an old and dying culture meets one that is vibrant and just beginning to live. The Stone Age man came too quickly into this twentieth century. Although he had spent those few years in association with "civilization," it had been a very peripheral joining. Joe had been an outsider during all those years. The man, like the boy, had never had a chance. These white Americans could accept the relatively familiar Irish, German, Swede, Italian, Chinese, Black man; these were concepts the European immigrants understood. Different customs and accents were a part of this melting-pot nation. But a true American conjured up many images. The great Indian wars of the Southwest were not yet history. The Little Big Horn and scalp-taking, war paint, and Geronimo had all become part of the new nation's vocabulary. The eastern part of the nation had only been "safe for settlers" for a little while in the 1850s. Joe told me that day, with no apologies, that he would always think of the Americans as "them." It took me many years, but I think I finally understand.

He had spent a great deal of time and effort trying to clarify these ideas for a mind too young to grasp them. I wanted to hear more. I thought I might understand the notions of "other" and "them" if he spoke of it longer, but the effort had weakened the ancient Indian. He seemed almost irritated as he waved me to silence. The story is long, he said, and you will only hear it if you listen. But then he smiled. I was sad to see the smile, because I could tell that it, like the anger, only covered his own pain. Joe went on, once again a young man in a distant place.

The way north was easy to travel. It was summer and food was available for one who knew how to find it. Some days the Indian would only walk a mile or less, stopped by some special thing. A clear pond called for a swim; a berry patch, for a meal. It was easy to go slowly. Joe was moving toward the mines, but going slower as he got closer. Although he knew he was doing this, it was not done on purpose. It just became easier, day by day, to find special things that could delay him. But one day, he asked at a farm and was told a mining company had begun operations recently, less than one day's walk to the north. Joe's summer of meadows and berries was about to end.

With the destination so near, Joe overcame his hesitation. He walked briskly, and near dusk, he was in sight of the pits. Two Trees hung back in the thick woods surrounding the coal mines and watched. His first impression was that everything was very dirty. Dust covered the rocks and even the tree leaves. There were three buildings. One was small, and a sign hung over the door. The sign was the only object Joe could see that wasn't a dingy, gray color. It, at least, was white. Joe blinked, the tiny sign gave little relief to this monotone landscape. He looked at the other two structures. They were both long, low, and uniformly gray. Two Trees noticed the wagon-wheel ruts in the mud around the buildings. They seemed to lead from the mouth of a cave in one large hill, to a road that led over another hill, and away from the mines. From his vantage he noted that even the water in the wheel tracks looked gray, or possibly black.

Joe felt it was too late in the day to enter the camp and ask for work, so he knelt in the lengthening shadows and kept watching. Just before it became too dark to see, he noticed motion near the cave. A man came out and stood pounding dust from his clothes. When he looked up, Joe saw that his face was the same gray color as everything else. Soon another man came out of the cave, then another. Eventually a large group had come out into the gathering gloom of dusk. He could hear them talking and laughing as they shook off the dust of the mine. They all drifted slowly into one of the long buildings. The

Indian saw lights wink on and flicker weakly through grimy windows.

Later, Two Trees heard a yell, and watched the men file out of the one long building into the other. Soon, laughs and the clanging sounds of pots and pans told him they were eating. This appealed to Joe Two Trees. A place where all sat together to eat and tell tales of the day could not be a bad place. This, after all, had been the Indian custom, too. Joe pulled his bear-skin around red shoulders to ward off the creeping chill of early autumn. He ate dried food from his pouch and thought about the things he might see the next day. Shortly, only night eyes watched. Bat, owl, raccoon were awake, but Joe slept soundly. He had reached the place the duck hunter had spoken about.

Long before the sun began to cast its feeble false-dawn light, Joe was already up. He rose quickly and sought out a small creek that he had crossed the day before. Here, he stripped and scrubbed the road grime from his body. His clothes were dirty and in poor repair, but they were the best he had. He resolutely walked toward the small building with its white sign.

Inside, a lantern burned and two men were hunched over a small desk. Joe could see them through a window as he neared the door. He knocked and one of the men turned toward the door. It opened and Joe was impaled upon a stare that lasted many seconds. The man looked him over from toe to head several times, his eyes coming to rest on Joe's face. At length, he growled, asking what Joe was doing there. The man's fierce attitude and nasty voice made Joe unsure for a moment. He almost turned and left, but he had come so far. He found his voice and stated his purpose, "I look for work."

The man laughed. He pointed to an object mounted on the wall above the desk, and asked if Joe recognized it. Joe said, "It is knife." The man grinned and answered, "No, it is saber." He explained that this very saber had killed many Comanches and Apaches over the years. He told Joe that he had been a cavalry officer for many years and had only recently retired and come east. Joe must have been quite baffled. He had never heard of a Comanche or an Apache. They were just strange-sounding names to the Indian. He looked again at the long saber. The rising sun, shining redly through the trees, glittered cold light off the polished steel. The Indian shivered involuntarily.

The boss, for Joe now saw that he was this, continued. He said he would as soon hire a "redskin" as a "nigger" because both had weak minds and strong backs. He glowered at Joe as he informed the Indian that he would happily kill him if he ever was given an excuse. Then he asked if Joe still wanted to work in the mines.

Two Trees was about to refuse but, he thought, he had fought for all that was his. True, that wasn't very much, but he had never retreated from any fight. There had been the thieves in New York, the bear, the winter's cold, even the fears within himself. He had always fought. So far, he had won. This man's offer was another challenge. Joe wanted to join the miners and eat in the long building with them.

Joe told the boss that he *did* still wish to work in the mine, and would be careful to give the man no reason for wanting to kill him. He hid any emotion and tried to appear very calm. The boss accepted it, and with no further preliminaries, gave Joe the name of the mine foreman. He directed Joe to enter the mine and tell that man to put him to work. There was no talk of pay, hours, or anything else. Joe left the office doorway and walked into the black mouth of an anthracite coal mine.

He walked along a low corridor of stone and dirt. The ceiling and walls were supported by timbers that formed a creaky lattice on both sides of him. Here and there water trickled down to drip on his head and clothing. At intervals, the yellow glow of lanterns lit the way. Between the pools of light stood gulfs of unthinkable black. Joe was reminded of the winter in the buried wigwam. But this darkness was different. It was windless but chilled, black but separated by tiny islands of light. The darkness was so deep as to be less a lack of light than a thing unto itself. He felt it as he walked from oasis to dull oasis. It settled in his hair and entered his body as he breathed.

Two Trees could hear noises somewhere ahead, so he went on. He sensed that the long tunnel had begun to slant downward, into the earth. Remembering old Algonquin stories about the evil spirits in caves within the earth, Two Trees shifted his bearskin burden and placed one hand on the handle of the flint knife inside his shirt. He didn't turn back, as all his instinct demanded. He went on, committed.

The man-made cave took a sudden turn to the left, and Joe

saw men. One stood under a lantern and issued orders to others who then scurried off into the murk. Joe walked bravely into the little circle of light.

He spoke the words the boss had told him. Very quickly he found himself swinging a pick axe near a man he could hardly see. The man sang a monotonous song in deep, husky tones, almost to himself. The work and singing went on and on. Periodically, a dull explosion sounded nearby. The ground would quiver and soon after, fine dust would drift into Joe's eyes and mouth. At last, Joe spoke. He asked the other miner what the noise was. Blasting in an attached shaft, he was told. Several more times during the sunless day, Joe tried to make conversation. He was answered, but no more. The singing seemed endless, but talk was brief. Joe didn't know if the rebuff was meant or only imagined. He continued smashing his pick into the rock in front of him. Sometimes he had to work kneeling down. When he had chopped out a certain amount of rock, other men would come with shovels and load it into carts. These, they wheeled toward the surface. When Joe thought that the song of few notes, and the dark, dust and cold would drive him crazy, it was over. He leaned his tool against the wall where the others had, picked up his bundle, and joined a line of blackened men. The line threaded its way from lantern to lantern, and finally out into cool evening air. The day's work was done.

Two Trees stood in the gathering dusk and beat dust from his clothes as the others did. He noticed, absently, that stars had started to appear above him. It seemed interesting, at least momentarily, that stars shone in the night above, but not below. Some of the men, those who lived nearby, went off into the trees and up the road. Suppers and wives, children and dogs waited in warm homes. The other men walked toward the long building. Joe followed. He thought it odd that no one seemed to notice him. He was just one more smudged miner, going to the bunkhouse. The anonymity lasted into the building, through a wash-up with water in buckets. Joe was dripping himself dry when one of the men walked up and spoke to him. Joe looked and was surprised. This man had washed, but his face was still coal black. The black man led Joe to a vacant bunk. It consisted only of several rough-cut boards, nailed together. Joe saw that, crude as it was, his bearskin would make it comfortable enough. The man informed Two Trees that he was called Cass, short for Cassius, a name given by his former owner. The Indian was very surprised at this mention of ownership. He asked the other how he could have been owned; he was not a horse or dog. Cass answered that he was, as several other miners here, an escaped slave. Thoughts of a farm where a door slammed on him leaped into Two Trees's mind. Again those words, "escaped slave," had come to him. This time he resolved to know their meaning.

A loud voice yelled from the darkness outside the barracks building. All the miners left and filed into the other structure, gray, long, but filled with warm, food smells. Joe found himself standing behind Cass on the line. Soon he was seated at a long, plank table with food in front of him. Cass joked that if it wasn't good, it was surely plenty. The Indian looked at his plate and was forced to agree with both statements. It was hot, though, and thinking of the man Cass, Joe didn't notice the taste. He asked the black man to tell him more about being owned. Cass told of a place named Georgia. He had worked, picking a crop called cotton, with several hundred other black slaves. They had been fed, clothed; in return they worked. When the field boss thought Cass wasn't working hard enough, or when the boss was mad for some other reason, he would beat the black man with a whip.

Cass had a wife for a time, but one day his owner had taken her to an auction and sold her. She had brought a high price because she was good at having babies. Without a mother, Cass's three little children had died. The oldest had only been three years old. The black man had not been able to do for them what a woman could. He worked in the fields from before sun to long after sun. Cass had buried his children all within less than half a year. Joe sat, amazed, but said nothing.

Cass went on, telling Joe about his old home over the sea. There had been many nations of black men such as he. Each held a place in that land, to hunt or farm. There were tribes and chiefs, medicine men and gods. Joe thought they must have been much like his own ancestors. Then men with guns and rum had come to kill, trade, or steal. They took people in any way that they could, or killed them. The unlucky ones, sold by their chiefs for rum, were crowded into small wooden ships and transported across the broad ocean, to be slaves in this country, as Cass was.

Cass went on. He told Joe that after a while, a white family had come to the cotton plantation. They taught the slaves more about the religion their masters had given them—a religion whose leader was named Jesus. The master had chased them at first. Later, he only laughed at them. He saw that they presented no threat to his business, and allowed them to come when they pleased. But the family had been a threat indeed. They told the slaves of a country called Canada. There, they said, slavery was not permitted, and all men were equal in the sight of God. If the slaves could get away, they could go to this country. Helpful white people would shelter them and send them on to the next stop. That, said Cass, was how he had escaped. They called this chain of havens "The Underground Railway."

The "railway" had not gotten Cass as far as Canada, though. Here, in Pennsylvania, he had been stopped. At each previous station, or stop along his route, Cass had been told of the next place to go. When he reached the mine, he had heard nothing else. This was the case with the other blacks here, too. They had gone this far, but here they stayed. It wasn't their choice. They worked, and were fed, but most thought it would be better to go on. True, no one beat them here, but in the cotton fields the work hadn't been this hard either. Here, men died in mine accidents. Their numbers were constant, however, since new slaves seemed to escape to the North regularly. This mine, however, was where the Underground Railway ended for them.

The older workers also knew of blacks who had been ordered into the office and never returned. Some even spoke of having seen the shiny saber come down from the wall. They only said these things in whispers. It was a well-known and carefully observed fact among the blacks that no one ever questioned the boss. No one ever watched too closely, or noticed various happenings. Doing this could bring the dreaded order to report to the office.

Joe spent several more days working in the ink-dark shafts, where it stayed night even at midday. He was near Cass sometimes in the darkness, and so they spoke. Joe began to realize that Cass was a kindly man. He was friendly, and cheerful, always making the best of his conditions. Joe asked if Cass had any plan for escaping to his old home, the place of the tribes. The black man told him it was impossible. The fate of escaped slaves who were caught was either to be shot, or whipped nearly to death and returned to their masters. It had been a difficult thing to escape, but to find a ship and try to return to Africa would be a sure way to be captured. Cass wasn't even sure that his tribal chief would accept him. The chief had freely sold him to the slavers in the first place. No. The mines were not a fine life, but at least here one could keep alive.

Joe felt himself becoming friends with the black man. The feeling itself was a strange one. Two Trees had never before had a friend. In all his life he had never known a child of his own age. He had never known a child at all, for that matter. During his small years, there had been a mother, a father, and Joe. When the parents had gone, he knew sorrow, but the loss had been somehow different. Joe had not had other relatives, an uncle, a brother, a grandfather, to talk to and console him. Until the age of fifteen, he had not heard a human voice except his parents'. When the parents had died, first the man and then the woman, Joe had no one. The sound of a voice became an alien thing, a thing to fear. After he left Hunter Island, Joe met farmers, hunters, bosses, and others, but none had ever been really a friend. Cass was becoming that. Joe didn't know of the word "friend," but the feeling of gladness that had begun to come into his life was teaching him.

During those first days Two Trees listened to the black man very carefully. The stories made a deep, biting impression. When he thought of the ships, the beatings, the cotton fields, Joe felt revulsion. If before he had regarded these Americans only as "others," now he was fast coming to see them differently. An element of horror was starting to intertwine itself within his conception of the white race.

The Indian thought back to his time in New York. He remembered Tony the shopkeeper. That man had been kind and good. He had done what he could to help the young boy. He had given much. Why, he wondered, had Tony not elicited these strange, new feelings? Joe considered the matter while he swung a pick axe, deep inside the earth. At length an answer began to form in his mind. It never found words. It was never expressed, but after a time, Two Trees knew that Cass, unlike Tony, could not read the talking words. As a shopkeeper, Tony had been one of the white man's creatures. Like dog, pig, cow, horse, Tony had been a part of their world. This was the world that Cass, subservient though he was, would never join voluntarily. Cass, like Joe, would accept their food, work, shelter, but never give over the thing that dwelt within him. There was a fierce, nearly animal part to both men that would never, could never be tamed. Joe realized this; like the bearskin, these things were, Joe knew, matters of the spirit.

Life at the mine began to form a routine. As the days went by, wake, work, eat, sleep became the new pattern of Joe's life. Days of rest from work were very infrequent. They were based solely on the needs of the mine. The needs or wants of the workers played no part. On the first day off, Joe had been resting in the barracks, talking to Cass. A white miner came in and told Joe that he was ordered to the office by the boss. Cass was very frightened for Joe, but knew there was little he could do. The black man suggested that Joe might run away, back to the woods. Joe thought for a moment, but decided he would not. That thing within him, that animal part of him, would not allow it. Trying very hard to seem brave, Joe started toward the office.

Before he reached to knock on the door, Joe's hand went to the hilt of the stone knife. Reassured by the feel of it, he knocked. The boss opened the door and stared coldly at Joe. It was almost as if time had run backward to their first meeting. After many unsettling seconds had passed, the white man curtly ordered Joe to take down the sign that hung over the door. Joe did, and the man asked if it was clean. He responded that it seemed so. The boss said he was wrong. The miner whose job it was to clean the sign each day had died and dust accumulated. Now, said the boss, the job belonged to Joe. Each morning, before work at the mine, Joe was to take the white sign down from its hooks and wash it. From the tone of his voice and expression of face, Joe could tell that the boss would be sure to examine the sign every day. Failure to clean it, even for one day, might be just the reason the boss had told about on the first day; the reason to kill him. Joe told the boss he would do his best. The man replied that it had better be good enough.

He slammed the door and Joe was left holding the sign. He tried brushing the coal dust off with his shirt sleeve, but it only smeared and looked worse than it had. The Indian put the sign under one arm and started off for the same creek he had used when he first came here. In its cold water, Two Trees dutifully washed the black dust from the sign. He walked back and hung it on the hooks.

When he returned to the barracks, Cass was relieved. They both knew that what they had silently feared had not come to pass. Joe had returned alive. He told Cass of the new job, and after discussing it, they agreed that it wouldn't be a great hardship. It meant rising a little earlier, but that would be only an inconvenience. The two men were surprised that this was all the boss had done to Joe. The retired cavalry officer's dislike of the Indian was no secret among the workers.

As winter wore on, the mystery slowly unfolded. Periodically, Joe was assigned to more "special" jobs. Joe washed dishes at the mess hall, chopped wood for the office stove, carried water and did all the other little jobs that no one else wanted. By spring, he was working nearly as many hours on these jobs as he was in the mines. The scheme was clear. The boss wanted to antagonize the Indian into giving him an excuse to kill him in "self-defense." Cass realized what was happening, and he would often talk to Joe, calming him. He told Joe that he must leave. The outcome of this test of wills was inevitable. One of the combatants would die. If it was the boss, police would come and then Joe would die. If it was Joe, no police would come. He would be buried secretly in the slag heaps, and forgotten. Joe saw the truth in Cass's words, but even though he knew he should leave, he didn't.

The staying was a strange thing. It was made up of many parts. Joe knew he was strong. The extra work, unpleasant though it was, would not kill him. In some way Joe even enjoyed the contest between him and the white boss. It contained an element of danger. Sometimes Two Trees felt like an animal must when it knows it is being hunted. The test sharpened his senses and his mind. These were not bad things. Gradually, Joe came to like the silent struggle. The man wanted to kill him, but Joe seemed always a step ahead. Then there was Cass. Cass was part of the reason for staying. If he had shown an interest in going, Joe would probably have left with him. Cass, however, was afraid to leave. So it went with the two friends, one afraid to go; the other afraid not to, but staying anyway.

Spring stretched into summer, then fall and winter. The seasons passed, almost unnoticed by the busy Indian. During this time, Joe had accepted each new job without complaint. He had done it carefully and well. He had given attention to even the smallest detail of every job. The Indian had done this because he knew it irritated the boss not to find fault in his work. The white man had never commented. There had been no "well done," or pat on the back, but slowly, a grudging look of respect had crept into his eyes. Now, when the boss spoke to Joe, he was a bit less nasty. There was never to be friendship between them, but at least the hatred was dying.

By the following summer, a strange transition was beginning. Just as Joe had originally been assigned to the various extra tasks, one by one he was relieved of them. Each was given to some other miner who had managed to find disfavor in the boss's cold eyes. When fall was painting the leaves of surrounding trees into a gaudy frame for the gray mine, Joe was working, as he had started, only at mining coal.

13

Indian Again

A war was coming. It had already begun in many subtle ways. News of its reasons had filtered even into the dark mine shafts. Slaves spoke of the war as one that would free them forever. Bosses spoke of it as one that would burn much coal in ships and factories. They all spoke as if the shooting had started, but it had not yet.

The friends talked about this coming war one night, and Cass told Joe as much as he knew of it. Joe could understand enough to see that it was bound to happen. Cass ended by saying that he and several other runaway slaves at the mine had decided to leave and volunteer their service in the Northern army. He asked Joe to join them. The Indian thought long and hard about Cass's proposition. But the next day he told Cass that while he wished him well, he would not go along. He thought too little of these white Americans to join in their war and do their fighting. There was no cowardice in Two Trees's decision and both men knew it. It was more because Joe, the native born, was even less "American" than Cass, from far away. Joe's ties were with the land itself, not with these men who had usurped it from his people. He would not be drawn among them by a war of their making.

Cass and the other slaves set the day for leaving and made their preparations quietly. They didn't know how the boss would react, so secrecy was kept. When the time came, Joe made his goodbyes and knew that he would feel the loss of his friend. As he watched them leave, he thought he knew how his ancestors had felt when they watched their clansmen go off to join the Iroquois. He almost went to join the slaves then, but something held him back.

When the men mustered for work in the morning, Joe was also gone. In the early, predawn hours he had wrapped his few belongings in the bearskin, and walked into the winter woods. Joe hadn't followed the others, he had set off to the north. By sunrise, many miles separated him from the coal mines. His spirits rose with each additional step. Later that day, Two Trees, the Indian, sat at a small fire and watched a rabbit roasting. The sight and aroma made him wonder why he had spent the time mining coal. But simultaneously he knew the answer. It had hardened and toughened him both physically and mentally. The experience had taught him much. The mine had been Joe's school, his education. He had learned many things about the white men and about himself. He now knew that they didn't want him on any but the most demeaning terms. He knew that equality between them and himself was at least as impossible as it was for the black slaves. He had learned to be hated, and to hate. But, he had also discovered friendship. On balance, thought Two Trees, the experience had been a valuable one. Then he looked off at a series of low ridges, which he would be crossing next day. Joe wondered what new feelings and sights were waiting there, in the wide world, for his discovery. It was good to be on the march again. That old familiarity with the road telegraphed through his shoes, warming him against the chill.

After he had eaten, Joe found a small pond and smashed away some ice. In the pool formed, he washed the coal dust from his clothing and body. When it was gone, he felt more a part of nature than in a long time. He sat shivering at his fire, wrapped in the bear robe, while his clothes dried. He didn't notice the cold though. Happiness was in his heart, warming him. It was the contentment of an Indian with a fire, an open sky above, and a full stomach.

Two Trees prepared himself a sleeping place and watched the night darken. Stars appeared and the sounds of night creatures stirred. Joe felt the natural darkness fold around him like a blanket. It was so different from the dark of the mines. It was clean and good. Joe found himself thanking his Maker for the night. Abruptly he realized that he had not thought about Tchi-Manitou for a long time. His mind had been too occupied with unimportant things. In striving to join the white world, Joe had begun to lose his Indianness. He had suspended himself to dangle between the two worlds. He had been unable to enter the new one, and unable to return to the old, dead one. That night he rediscovered his heritage, never to lose it again. Joe thought himself the last of his kind, but still he decided that what years might lie ahead would be spent, in thought and deed, as an Indian.

When dawn came, he was up and on his way. Two Trees didn't know exactly where he was heading, but the lure of the land had taken its hold on him. Each river called out to be crossed; each mountain cried to be climbed. A magnetism drew him along like the needle on a compass. But unlike the needle, Joe turned, after many weeks, away from his northerly course. He had reentered New York State, probably somewhere near what is now Port Jervis. The land of woods and mountains was a place of great beauty, but for some reason, he turned toward the rising sun and continued in its direction.

The turning was a great pity. Had Joe continued to the north, it is very possible that he might have eventually wandered into one of the Iroquois reservations in upstate New York. Joe didn't know it, but the Iroquois confederacy still survived. Had he gone north, the Indian might well have found a place in the world among his own. He might have lived there and prospered, possibly even meeting distant relatives, born across the generations into his time. But fate turned his feet that day, and in so doing locked his destiny upon him. Thereafter, he was Joe Two Trees, last of his kind.

Here I stopped Joe. I knew now that he was unaware of the existence of other Indians anywhere. I needed time to figure out how, and if, I should tell him. The fire had burned low and I made much of rebuilding it. Then I brought water for more tea. All the while I debated silently. Would it make Joe happy to know that other children of the Maker still lived on? Or would the knowledge that he had so nearly found them make him bitter, suddenly hating all that had been his life? The man was

*sick, dying. Would this revelation destroy him? From the way he
looked, I knew that it, or anything else, was very unlikely to save
him. I hung on the horns of dilemma, vacillating and trying
hard to look busy. Joe gazed into the fire and seemed not to
notice me. I handed him his tea and sat again. He took the cup
with trembling hand and looked at me. "What is it that you
must tell me?" The decision had been taken from my hands.*

*I gently explained to Joe that some Indians had indeed sur-
vived into the twentieth century. I said that although he was the
last Bronx Algonquin, his kind was not yet dead. Joe listened
very seriously to what I had to say. I imagine now that all sorts of
things were going through his mind. There were the things that
might have been, and never were, and never again could be.
There were the years upon years of loneliness that needn't have
happened at all. The chance for a wife and children had existed,
but Joe had never known it. When I finished, Joe continued
staring into the flames, and although his expression never wa-
vered, tears were streaming down both of his cheeks. Later he
thanked me for telling him. He said that it made no difference
anymore. The past was a thing that no man, white or Indian,
could ever change. We sat together for a time, and Joe rested,
trying to call up failing strength and continue his story.*

Through that winter and into the spring, he wandered in the
mountains of New York. Two Trees passed towns and farms,
but he avoided them all. The land was good and he caught or
found enough food. That winter was a mild one. Little snow fell
where Joe went, and life was not difficult. Joe wondered, that
winter, about the black soldier named Cass. He was never to
see him again, but he hoped that Cass would win the freedom
he so desired.

By late summer, Two Trees reached the shores of a large
body of water. When the morning mist cleared, he could see the
far shore. Later that day he saw a boat pass and remembered it
as one he had seen in New York. He realized then that he had
almost made a complete circle since Hunter Island of years ago.
It was the river he had crossed once before.

On making this discovery his thoughts went to Tony, the
almost-friend of long ago. Joe had thought about him frequently during the years in Staten Island, New Jersey, and

Pennsylvania. Surely, sufficient time had passed. By now, he wouldn't be remembered in the city. It should be safe to return. Should he follow the river along this bank and cross when he was opposite the city? Perhaps he should cross here and proceed downstream on the far side. But it was so pleasant in the spot where he was. The reed-surrounded lagoon nearby offered excellent prospects for a swim. Fall was forcing summer aside, and all the nature signs told Joe to beware of a winter with much snow. The woolly-bear caterpillar had grown extra fur, the wasps had built their nests high above ground, the squirrels had bushier tails than in other years. Yes, a prudent Indian would give thought to preparing his winter place. In the end, Joe decided to walk neither shore. He would do the prudent thing, and decide in spring.

But before spring, or winter for that matter, there was still fall. It was that time of warm, gold-hued days, and Joe took full advantage of it. Plans for winter quarters could wait another day. He stripped to his red skin and dove into clear, warm water. The river was still virgin here. There was no city nearby to dump its filth into the water. This stretch was closer to the river's distant source, a lake that would later be named "Tear of the Clouds." Joe swam and paddled until he began to feel chilly in the running water. He climbed onto a flat rock and dried in the warm breeze. He watched the peaceful water slip past him and looked around at the screening reeds. The Maker must have had him, and this day, in mind when he created the small lagoon. Joe knew he had chosen the right course. New York City could wait a season longer.

Joe's spot was almost perfect for a winter encampment. The west and north sides were flanked by high bluffs. The river would ensure that no one could approach unseen from the front. On the south, fruit trees stood, ready for Joe's picking. Under the trees there was thick brush, ideal rabbit cover. Beyond the trees there appeared to be low, clear land, but Joe hadn't explored that area yet. The weather was still quite warm, and time might remain to catch and smoke fish. The prospect of dried fish for the winter larder was not an unpleasant one.

Before fall had begun, probably by early September, Two Trees had finished his home building and the better part of his provision gathering. A few miles upstream he even managed to hunt and kill a large deer. The skin meant new buckskin clothes, the flesh would be dried. Many winter meals were now ready. Joe fished along the river with spear and gorge and caught kinds of fish he had never seen before. Soon, he was well prepared for any winter that might blow down upon him.

14

The Red-Haired Woman

Joe was satisfied with his work. On the sunlit day that it was done, a swim was in order. He shed his clothing at the new wigwam's entrance and walked the short distance to his lagoon. As he approached the tall reeds, he heard splashing. Joe thought it might be a large fish or ducks, and he continued quietly so he wouldn't frighten off whatever had entered the protected spot. Slowly, he approached the edge and parted the growth enough to peek through unseen. The source of the splashing was readily apparent. At the middle of the lagoon, with brilliant red hair fanned out around her head, floated a woman. As he watched, she dove under the surface and disappeared. Joe had just begun to feel concern when she suddenly popped up again in the shallow water. Two Trees felt some embarrassment and thought that he should probably leave, but something deep inside kept him where he was. He had never really known a woman except his mother, and now he was watching one at her bath. He had listened at the mine, to the men. They had often talked about women and the things men and women could do together. Joe had learned that the body of a woman could bring great pleasure to a man. He stayed in his concealment and watched her splash around in the clear shallows. Once, she turned directly toward him and stood up. He was frightened that she might have seen him, but she gave no sign, so he sat still and continued to watch. The water was clear and only up to her milk-white thighs. The Indian was surprised to see that she was truly a woman of reddish hair. It was the color of the sundown sky that heralds a fair day to come. It was the color of maple leaves and Virginia creeper when frost first touches them.

The woman finished her swim and walked out onto the sandy beach. There she climbed up on the flat rock Joe had used and lay down, folding her arms under her face. The rear view impressed Joe as much as the front had. There is no question that this was an erotic experience for Joe. He had never had a woman, but the condition of his body at that moment told him that he would, given a chance, easily figure out how it was done.

She rose, walked to a pile of clothes, and dressed. As she did, Joe thought he noticed her glance quickly at his hidden location, but he couldn't be sure. She went off through the fruit tree wood and was soon out of sight.

The Indian stayed where he had been hidden and waited. When he was sure she was gone, he stood up and hurried back to his camp. There he dressed quickly and trotted off toward the trees to pick up her trail. He found it easily and followed it. As he went along, he wondered what he would do if he came face to face with her. The great sexual excitement running through his blood was urging him on; but to what? Joe knew he could easily overpower the young woman, but he knew that was a bad thing. If he found her, he wouldn't know what words to say to endear himself. Would he find her as exciting wearing clothing as he had when she was naked? All these conflicting thoughts conspired together to bring him back to a more normal condition. Slowly, his burning excitement softened to become a dull yearning.

Two Trees walked on, following the trail. Where the trees ended, he stood in their shadows and looked across a short expanse of clear ground. There stood a small log farmhouse. Joe was surprised that he hadn't learned it was here until now. He hadn't expected any farms to be this far from a town, so he hadn't really looked, and most of his hunting had been upriver. He studied the farm. It was small and had a seedy look of disuse. The house needed repairs, and the fields were untended. Only a small patch had been plowed and planted. Although now turned over to grass, the overgrown furrows indicated they had once been meant for food crops. A few chickens wandered around, pecking up any food they happened across. Several pigs wallowed in a rickety pen. From the look of the rails, Joe was sure they probably entered and left at will. He imagined that they must forage in the nearby woods for food.

As he was completing his visual survey a sound caught his attention. The door hinge creaked dryly and a red-haired woman came out to the porch. From his distance, Joe couldn't see her features, but her proportions told him she was the woman from the water—he had already had ample opportunity to memorize these. She looked first one way, then the other, as if she expected someone. Then she turned and reentered the cabin. It was late in the day, and Joe started back to his shelter. Now that he knew where she lived, he would go home and consider this strange, new situation. His great prowess, killing a bear, surviving against often tremendous odds, none of these had prepared him to deal with a woman.

That night, confusion kept sleep away from the sheltered wigwam for many hours. Exciting, conflicting thoughts kept the Indian awake. The bearskin, which had always been sufficient in the past, now seemed to lack a certain warmth. Once, he had almost decided to get up and walk to the small farm. But, he thought, he might be shot for a wild animal raiding the livestock. Anyway, he had no idea of what he would do when he reached the farm. He stayed at his camp. The sleep that finally overcame Joe Two Trees was a troubled one. Confused it found him, and confused he still was, when it left.

In the morning Joe stayed late near his wigwam. He made breakfast and sat near the hut doing nothing. This was unusual for the man. He was a person of activity. During all the hours of light, he did, even if nothing needed doing. In his philosophy waste was evil. Even the waste of the light, given by his Maker, was not allowed. This day, Joe did not do, he sat. He was waiting. I doubt that he realized it but he was waiting for the sound of splashing.

While the old man told me this part of his story, there were frequent pauses. Some of these were due to his growing weakness, but others, I can now tell in retrospect, were due to his choosing the right words to explain these things to an eleven-year-old boy.

*During the telling of what was a powerful emotional experience
in his life, he never used a word that we would call "dirty." All of
his descriptions were couched in terms of natural beauty, which
would approach being poetry if I could remember exactly how he
phrased them. He was telling me of growing first love.*

Toward the middle of the afternoon, the splashing finally
came. Joe walked toward the screening growth of bulrushes
and cattails. He hoped that he would not find ducks or fish. If
there had been ducks, they were gone when Joe cautiously
parted the stalks. The only life in the lagoon was a red-haired
nymph. To Joe, she was quite enough. Joe watched as she swam
and washed. He was fascinated, not only by her nudity, but by
her beauty. From the description he gave me, she must have
been a very lovely woman indeed, or at least he saw her as
such.

Joe continued to watch from his spot, and she seemed almost
to be offering herself. The frequent turns toward his hiding
place, the way she held her full breasts up with her hands,
seemed to say that she knew he was there. Yet, she made no
overt sign. Joe didn't know if he had been discovered but felt
that since she made no objection he might as well stay. The
swim lasted longer today. She seemed to be dragging out each
movement, making it more tantalizing than it was yesterday.
Could it possibly be that she was not doing all this on purpose?

She left the water. Again she sunned on the convenient rock.
This time though, she didn't lie still as on the previous day. She
rolled and turned almost continually, as if anxious to expose
her every part to sun; or could it have been to view? None of
this of course was lost on Joe. The unfamiliar feelings were
back in force. He was tempted, several times, to walk into the
clearing and make his presence known. He didn't do it, fearing
she might scream or run away.

Again, as she had a day earlier, the woman dressed herself.
But she did it slowly, methodically. Somehow, the most intimate parts of her body always seemed to face toward the hidden Indian. When she was finished, she walked slowly back
through the trees. Joe followed again, but stopped in the shadows once more. He watched the cabin for a time and finally the
door opened. Instead of the woman a dog sauntered onto the

porch and lay down in a patch of late afternoon sunlight. The dog was lean and gray. Its gaunt shoulders and hips spoke of poor feedings, but its low-slung belly told of more mouths coming soon to be fed. Joe watched a while longer, until he saw the long shadows creeping across the field. By then he was sure that the object of his adoration would be seen no more that day. He walked back to the wigwam near the protecting cliff face.

That night, it was not only the bearskin that lacked warmth. The whole hut seemed an empty place. It was once more the loneliness of the time when his parents had died. Only now there was nothing vague in the deep yearning for company. Joe knew exactly whose company he desired. The Indian spent another night with little prospect of sleep's comfort. Before dawn, while it was still quite dark, he dressed and climbed the high bluff behind his camp. When he had gained the top, he rested his back against a convenient tree and watched the moonlit river slide silently along below. Joe watched the harvest moon set. As it neared the tree-lined horizon, it grew in size and beauty. The bright white of its light was suffused by a golden cast that faded into red. Just before the moon sank into the far-off trees, its color was that of the woman's hair.

Sometime near dawn Joe must have dozed off. He woke with a start, to the realization that it was already midmorning. Two Trees ran to the edge and looked down into the lagoon. No one was there. Had he overslept and missed her? Joe scrambled down the steep rocks to his hut. He ran to the beach. An absence of wet footprints reassured him. Returning to the camp, he sat to wait for the sound of splashing. He sat, waiting and feeling very foolish. Something kept him there though, and foolish or not, he kept on waiting.

As the hours passed, he thought she wouldn't come. Today, she must be doing other things. Perhaps she would not swim any more now that the weather was growing cooler. A hundred possible reasons presented themselves to Joe's mind. Then he heard a splash and his spirits soared. He trotted to the brushy spot and went silently to its edge. She was there, and as usual, her lush body had its instantaneous effect on Joe. He settled down into the deep grass, and prepared to follow her every movement with his eyes. He had been there only for a short time when an odd thing happened. She swam directly toward his hidden spot. Joe was surprised, but stayed where he was. Soon she was floating directly in front of him. She calmly looked at the bushes which hid him and asked if he wouldn't rather come out and join her for a swim. Then she headed back toward the center of the enclosed pool.

Having been discovered, Joe stood up and stripped. After all, one does not go swimming with his clothes on. He dove in and swam tentatively toward the naked girl. Although the clear water made it impossible for her to overlook his excitement, she chose to ignore it. They talked of minor things, the weather, the water. After some time she said she had to leave and suggested that Joe come to visit her sometime, saying something about being bored and lonely. As the red-haired beauty left the water and walked up the beach, she made no effort to cover or hide herself from Joe's eyes. The man realized that he hadn't asked her name. By that time she was dressing, and he hesitated. She finished and walked off in the direction of the weedy farm. Joe stood, still waist deep in the water, and watched her disappear. He was quite undecided about what he should do next.

He turned, gathered the clothing that had been dropped on the reedy bank, and returned to his shelter. Once there, he started a small fire and prepared food for himself. These things were all accomplished in mechanical, detached fashion. Joe's conscious thoughts were occupied with different matters.

He had little experience with women, and in matters of intimacy, none whatsoever. The woman's young body and the few words that passed between them had plucked a string buried somewhere in his depths. In some hidden corner of his being, some place that he hadn't ever known existed, an unlearned knowledge was announcing itself. In all his young years, Joe had so far been too occupied with survival to give thought to reproduction. Then, a chance encounter in the woods had changed that in a matter of days. Hormones that had, till then, combined with the adrenaline of "fight or flight" to strengthen his muscles for life-or-death encounters now flowed wildly to other body parts. Those parts were receptive. As in all mammals, Joe's warm blood carried certain instincts that, taught or not, would eventually make their way through the body into the brain. Joe thought then of sexual pleasures and delights. He knew little of them except from the miner's talk, but he wanted to find out.

This, however, was only a veneer, covering his true need. Joe was experiencing the human desire to re-create himself, to pro-create, to continue his kind. The Indian wanted a child, per-haps a son. A small boy who could learn the things Joe had to teach would be an infinitely desirable product of an equally desirable coupling. The boy could learn all the natural lore from Two Trees, and the white man's ways from the red-headed woman, mother. Joe's thought progression had already reached a point where he believed that all this was certain to occur. Now, only the details of wooing the mother-to-be re-mained. After all, thought the Indian, he had already met her and she had not run off or rejected him in any other way. She had even said he could come to see her. Surely, these were all signs that she felt as he did. Then too, there was something he had missed since the death of his mother. It was the warmth of a female's ways. Joe had often noticed how his mother had done special things, small things, for Eagle Feather, to make him happy. Until he died, she had tried to please him in all ways. The concept of wife-mother was tied up in Joe's mind along with remembered smells of cooking food and the feel of gentle caresses. Yes, his life force was saying, as it was for your father, so should it be for you. Unfortunately, none of these lofty thoughts led Joe to question the obvious contradiction. Why was a beautiful, white girl living alone in a desolate woods in the first place?

Joe finished the food and dressed. He looked around for something to bring as gift, and chose pieces of his dried deer meat. He set off for the house past the fruit trees. This time, he only hesitated briefly at the edge of the tree line, then contin-ued into the open field. As he neared the rough cottage, the dog barked at him several times. At this he stopped to be sure it would not rush down from the porch and attack. Joe decided that the dog was so heavy with the new life of puppies that she would not do much rushing, so he walked on. Then the door opened, and the woman came out. The dog's warning sounds must have called her away from cooking, because she carried a ladle with her. Joe stopped again, unsure of himself. But she smiled, so he held out the meat and said he had brought it for

her. He could tell that she was quite pleased. She said she
would add his meat to the stew she was just then cooking, and
he was welcome to join her for supper. Joe readily accepted.

There was a small matter though; she pointed to an axe and
asked if he would cut more wood for the fire. Joe started immediately. He was glad of an excuse to stay near the woman and
still not have to think about things to say. Soon, he had
chopped enough wood to last her for several days. When she
heard that he had stopped chopping, she came out again. The
amount of wood apparently pleased her. She waved for him to
come in and stayed in the doorway as he did. This afforded Joe
the pleasant sensation of brushing against her body as he
passed. Then she gently squeezed his arm, as if saying that she
hadn't been offended by it.

The smell of cooking food was a welcome one. Even though
he had recently eaten, it was only little and roughly prepared.
The kitchen smells of real pot-and-pan cooking, combined with
the warmth of a log cabin, reassured Two Trees about the ideas
of wife and mother. She hurried about, doing one thing and
then another, so conversation was still not required. Joe
appreciated this and the opportunity it gave to examine the
interior.

The house had only one large room. On one wall was a
fireplace with a large kettle suspended within. Other pots and
utensils hung along that wall. The opposite end of the room
was partially screened off by several blankets hanging from a
rope that stretched from the front wall to the back. Behind the
blankets was a large, quilt-covered bed. The foot end of the bed
extended past the blanket screen. The floor at the bottom of the
bed was carpeted with, of all things, a bearskin. He looked
again. He couldn't be mistaken, even in the poor light. It was a
bearskin. He looked at other aspects of the room. Over the door
was a rack that held two guns. One was a shotgun, the other a
rifle. There was a third space on the gun rack, but it was empty,
almost as if someone had picked out one weapon and gone
hunting. The bearskin, the guns, these were all man things. As
Joe looked further, he noticed other signs that a man either
lived here or had only recently. He said nothing, hoping the
mystery would untangle itself as time went by.

The girl announced that she was ready, and smiling, led Joe

to the table by his hand. They sat and Joe saw the meat he had brought. Although it was actually the center of the meal, she had done things with vegetables and bread to make the whole appear a sumptuous feast. Joe tasted and was pleasantly surprised. He hadn't eaten cooking like this since his farm days on Staten Island, and that was some years ago. Since then, there had been the bleak mine mess hall, or his own sparse forest rations. Both would keep a body alive, but only that. The woman-cooked meal was a wondrous thing to Joe Two Trees, man of the wilderness trails.

The woman had been bantering for some time with words of little importance. These required a smile or a short word in answer, and this suited Joe. He was still finding his tongue. The ideas of being invited in, eating supper, and sitting this close to the woman were all exciting, but also a bit frightening. It had come about so fast. This was not like fighting a man or a bear. Joe would feel little fright under those conditions of encounter. But the small beauty across from him was a quarry with which he had no experience. Then she said her name, Sheila, and asked his. Joe looked at her eyes. They were as blue as any sky he had ever seen. This surprised him, and for a moment he forgot that she had spoken. He was so intent on looking into her blue eyes that he forgot everything. She brought him back by joking that everyone else she had ever met had a name. He blurted out that he was called Joe. This seemed to be enough; she asked for no other name, and he gave none. Something had happened, though, in saying the name. Joe had overcome his discomfort and thereafter, talk became easier between them.

Soon, Joe was talking to her as he had talked to no one else before. He told her of his travels, his mining years, and many of his adventures. She seemed to be genuinely interested, so he went on. His origins and the killing in New York were things he kept to himself. She hadn't asked what he was, so she either didn't know, or knew and didn't care. He realized that his Indian heritage was often distasteful to whites, so he didn't volunteer that information. He also knew that mention of the killing, unintended though it had been, might frighten her off. When he felt that she was enjoying his talk, he probably started to boast a bit. It was his prowess as a hunter that the girl seized upon. She directed his talk to that and seemed impressed. A

shortage of fresh meat was one of her major problems. If Joe
saw fit to help her with that, she could be very appreciative. As
she said this, the arch of her eyebrows and tone of her voice
made him want to race out and hunt red meat. He knew he
would soon do just that.

The time had passed quickly, and too soon Joe realized that
it was late. He didn't know how to bring the subject from con-
versational matters to other things, and she had not done so for
him. He had recognized a certain overtone to her looks and talk
several times that seemed to suggest more than they had arrived at, but he had not known how to capitalize on it. He
thanked her for the meal and prepared to leave. This matter
would require thought at the wigwam. She asked Joe not to
forget her if he happened to go hunting. He quickly promised
he would not. Again she stood in the doorway and made him
squeeze his body past hers. The glow caused by that contact
lasted along the path, back to his shelter.

Lying in the shelter, he thought back over the whole event.
He considered various things to say when they met again. All
in all, he felt quite good about the meeting. He would hunt and
bring her game. She was sure to see his ardor. Suddenly the
other thought came back to Joe. There had been man-things in
her house. Whose? He hadn't asked and she hadn't said anything about another man. This was a matter that required further investigation. He didn't want to ask her, but his curiosity
was so great that he knew he must. If she didn't clarify this, he
would. He thought about the hunting for a while, and just as
sleep overtook him, Joe had a dream composed of the two
thoughts. He was hunting for meat in the dream, but as he
followed the trail to his quarry, he found not deer but a man.
The man had taken his beautiful Sheila, and he kept fleeing
with her, always out of Joe's reach. The dream became more
confused as it went on, until dawn came and relieved him of it.

Joe rose early and went upriver to check his snares and build
new ones. He had set enough to guarantee food for himself, but
now he was hunting for two. He cleaned the rabbits that were
already caught, and walked farther into the marshes up ahead.
He was looking for deer signs. Rabbits were good to eat, but
venison would make a more impressive gift. After searching for
a while, he came across the tracks of a large deer. Joe followed

these down toward the river. The muddy ground showed many tracks, all made by the same animal. This was the watering spot of a big buck deer. Joe recognized the pattern of footprints. This animal came here daily, probably at dusk, and drank. It was the reliability of such an animal, to form a pattern and live by it, that made him easy prey. In the woods the deer's keen senses would alert him to any move made by a man. In the open the deer could easily outdistance even the fastest human runner. But here, a prisoner of his pattern, the deer would eventually come to drink. This was when Joe would have the advantage.

He disturbed the deer's spot not at all and walked a good distance away. He searched until he found a young hickory sapling. Joe cut it and, as he had with the spear for his bear, sharpened the end into a long point. He built a small fire and hardened the wood in its flames. Then he walked back, keeping on the lookout for his deer. Joe didn't want it to see him yet. If the plan worked, he would be the last thing the deer ever saw, but that would be later. When he reached the drinking place, Joe noted the wind. It came from the north. He hid himself behind a low bush just south of the deer's pathway. Here, spear in hand, Joe hid and waited.

I had seen him do that trick at Hunter Island, and so, as he spoke of it, I could visualize the scene. Joe must have crouched and sat back on his legs. He would have been invisible as he stayed perfectly motionless, a part of the bush. He had arrived many hours too early, but that was for a reason. The passing time allowed Joe's scent to dissipate from the area, and blow away on the wind. I doubt that any white hunter could sit motionless for so long. To Joe it was natural.

So he crouched and waited, outwardly dead, unmoving, but with his mind racing. Thoughts of the deer gave over, when he knew he was all ready for it, to thoughts of Sheila. It was her bath time. The height and angle of the sun told Joe that several miles downriver, ripples and splashing now broke the smooth surface of a hidden lagoon. He was glad that the deer had given him an excuse to be here instead. Joe knew he could no longer hide in the bushes to watch the woman bathe. He was unsure of what her reaction would be if he brazenly showed up to swim. After all, he could no longer hide behind the pretext, however thin, of an accidental arrival. He knew, and she now knew he was aware of the fact that she would be naked. If he arrived at the lagoon dressed, she might think he was uninterested or silly. If he arrived nude, she might take it as an insult or a vulgar suggestion. It was better to be here, waiting for the deer to come. The other thing would solve itself in time. If that time produced a deer for Joe to carry to her, the solution might be a very favorable one for him.

As the shadows began to lengthen, Joe's ears strained to listen for any indication of the deer. Now and then a bird or small animal made tiny noises, but Joe's ear easily identified these and shut them out. It was nearly dark now, and the deer had not yet arrived. Perhaps it had found a better place or scented Joe's presence. It could have been ambushed by a hunter even quieter than the Indian. The spring of a silent mountain lion had ended the lives of many a deer. But Joe continued to wait, and he was finally rewarded. A movement in the bushes and the raucous screams of a bluejay told the Indian what he wanted to know. The long vigil hadn't been wasted.

The deer stopped out of Two Trees's thrusting range. The big animal hadn't survived the perils of its environment long enough to grow as large as it had by being careless. It sniffed and looked around. It was as if it suspected something.

Joe started to worry. Had he left some visual or scent sign of his presence? Would the powerful legs spring, carrying the deer off and away? The buck stood motionless for a long time, but in the end it decided to continue toward the river. Joe was relieved, but no motion gave a hint of it. Not the smallest breath or wink of eye revealed his presence. The animal browsed slowly along its usual path until it came parallel with the hidden Indian. When the distance was perfect, Joe's legs exploded like steel springs, sending him through the curtain of bush. His spear entered the buck's side, slid between its ribs, and went deep into the chest cavity. The startled creature, unexpectedly hurt, jumped high into the air. When it fell, it stumbled, momentarily losing footing. It quickly rose though, and dashed off leaving a wide trail of bright red blood. Joe's spear had not entered the heart as he had expected. The deer was badly hurt, but it would not soon fall dead.

The hunter was faced with a serious problem. If the deer wasn't mortally wounded, it might wander a long distance before it found a place to lie down. If he let this happen, a wildcat or even dogs might deprive him of his kill. Tracking the animal in darkness would be a difficult business, even dangerous. If he came upon the buck suddenly in the dark, it might use those sharp antlers as a last defense. But if he did not follow, chances were he'd lose the deer. Joe decided quickly. The danger and discomfort of night tracking after a wounded animal were small when compared to the prospect of having no gift of venison for Sheila.

Two Trees set out by the light of a rising half-moon. Often, he was required to crawl from one blood patch to the next in order to maintain his trail. After he had followed for a long time, Joe came upon the deer. It had lain down to rest and snorted loudly as he approached. It rose stiffly to its feet and stood facing Joe. He reached for his knife, thinking the wounded beast planned to make a stand. Instead, it whirled and dashed away. Joe saw only the white, flaglike tail bob up and down as the buck was lost to sight.

When the deer turned to escape, the spear which still hung from his side had caught on a branch and been yanked loose. Now the blood came much faster than it had. The trail led Joe several miles farther north. Soon, the moon set behind western trees, but the dull glow of predawn was starting to show in the east. With the light, Joe saw the quantity of blood that marked the buck's trail. He would soon be too weak to go on. The Indian slowed his pursuit to give the blood loss time to do its work. The strategy was sound, and a few hundred yards farther the deer lay unable to go on. Joe approached carefully, but the animal was far too weak to fight by then. The Indian finished it quickly with his knife.

A warm, autumn sun had risen above the thick trees by then, and Joe looked around. The trail he followed the night before had been a winding, roundabout one. He decided to climb a nearby hill and see if he could find a better way to return. It was tough climbing as he scaled the first half of the steep, wooded rise, but then the ground cleared and his trip to the top went quickly. He looked down into a deep valley on the other side and was surprised to see a small village. In the opposite direction he saw the sparkle of sun shining on water. It was the river. Mentally plotting his course, he returned to the deer and dressed it out. Joe skinned the animal and wrapped as much meat as he could carry inside the skin. He made a tow harness with two thin saplings and started back, skidding the burden behind him.

The tiny village, really no more than a collection of eight or ten log houses, interested Two Trees. He added it to his mental image of the area that surrounded his chosen winter quarters. When he arrived here from the west, Joe had seen no sign of human habitation. Then he had found Sheila's farm. Now this village. The area wasn't quite as deserted as it had seemed at first. These facts didn't worry the Indian, but they did put him on his guard. The village meant men, surely hunters. That was probably why the buck had been so cautious yesterday. These hunters would have guns. Joe decided it would be a good idea to hunt downriver in the future. There was another reason, too. The Indian had no desire to meet these whites. They were all unpredictable at best. He would not hunt where they did and hoped they would stay to the north. He fervently wanted the men from the village to keep their distance from his wigwam, his lagoon—and his Sheila. The last popped into his mind quite unexpectedly. Then he considered the possibility that the man-things in Sheila's home might belong to one from the village. Suddenly he hated the entire town, just on the off chance that his suspicion might be true. Joe Two Trees was, for the first time, jealous. He picked up his pace. He had been away for almost two days. It was too long.

Joe reached the river and turned downstream. It was easy travel there. The trees were thinner, and there were animal trails through the undergrowth. He reached the lagoon shortly. He didn't bother to stop at his wigwam, but proceeded through the trees and toward the farm. Again, the dog barked as he left the tree line. Her emaciated body was in such contrast to her enormous belly that he marveled at the fact that her pups had not yet been born. Her bark brought Sheila to the porch. Joe felt a warm spark blaze up within his chest. As he approached she asked why he had not met her for a swim the previous day.

Joe was very happy at this. The problem of whether he was welcome at the lagoon had just solved itself, as he had hoped it would while he waited for the buck. He walked toward her with his heavy gift.

In answer to her question, Joe pointed to the blood-soaked bundle tied between the sapling runners and told her he had gone hunting for meat. She came down and lifted a flap away. All the meat inside was dressed and well cut into choice portions. Sheila smiled broadly and asked if it was for her. Joe said it was, but that he hoped to be asked to share it. She looked at him and said he surely would be asked. She noticed the caked blood on Joe's hands and arms, mixed with dust and grime from the long walk. Sheila suggested that he go to the river and wash while she prepared the meat for drying. Just then the dog came down, sniffed at the bundled meat, and looked up longingly at the man. The look of hunger in her eyes moved Joe to take his flint knife and cut a large piece. He held it out and the dog eyed the red offering, but would not take it. Then Joe squatted down to the dog's level, and she carefully took it from his hand. Before she walked off to eat the meal, the skinny animal looked long and curiously at him. Joe wondered why the dog seemed afraid of him. He had never hurt her. Had some other man?

Joe looked at himself and silently agreed that a good washing should definitely be his next activity; and the sooner the better. The hungry flies of fall were making him uncomfortable. He turned and set out briskly for the clean water. When he got to the sandy beach, he stripped off his blood-spattered clothing and soaked them in water. Then he pounded the jacket and trousers on a rock until the water that he wrung out of them was clean. The cloth clothes were quite threadbare, and he mentally noted that he had better start on buckskin replacements. He now had two good hides. After he cleaned the new skin, thought Joe, he would make the winter clothes. He stretched his laundry over some low bushes to dry and walked into the water to complete his bath.

The man rubbed clean sand over his entire body and chilly water washed off the dirt that had covered his skin. He soon tingled all over from the abrasive grit and cool water. Feeling fresh and invigorated, he stroked to the center of the pool and floated there, enjoying the gentle tug of current against his body. In the protected backwater, only small fingers of tide could enter. While the powerful river drove past just a few feet away, the lagoon experienced only a gentle, circular flow. It was peaceful and lulling. Joe relaxed, nearly sleeping, in the shallow water. His mood was suddenly broken by a disturbance. He looked and was pleased to see the red hair of Sheila as she swam out to him.

Sheila stopped near the man and asked if he would like her to help him wash. Joe responded that he was already washed. The woman seemed insulted, and Joe didn't understand what he had done to cause this reaction. She asked if he didn't find her attractive. He hastened to assure her that he did. Nude as she was, he found her not only attractive, but irresistible. She wanted to know why, if he found her attractive, he did not want her to wash him. Naively, Joe hadn't seen the obvious connection yet. Seeing, though, that it seemed important to Sheila, he said he would be pleased to be washed by her. Joe let his feet sink to the bottom and the two stood facing each other, separated by only the water. Sheila reached down and gently began to wash him. He discovered immediately that he had misunderstood her intentions until that moment. The washing had been very much connected with the question of her attractiveness. Feeling Joe's excitement, she asked if he wouldn't like to wash her in return. Soon the two were exploring each other completely and thoroughly. Joe wanted more, and he made his needs known to her. By then, she wanted the same thing. They left the water and gathered their clothing. Not bothering to put it on, they ran toward the cottage together.

She drew him to the blanket-screened bed, and he felt the warmth increase as their two bodies blended into one. Joe noticed with a small part of his mind that he seemed to know exactly what to do. Where he was doubtful, her hands urgently directed him. After what could have been either minutes or hours, they lay side by side enveloped in a rosy afterglow. Joe's newfound knowledge showed him the miners had not exaggerated these pleasures at all. Sheila reclined quietly, a small smile on her face. Joe watched the rhythmic rise and fall of her breasts. He could tell that she was pleased, relaxed, and this added to his own pleasure.

Joe wanted to talk but he waited, not wishing to disturb the woman. She stirred and rolled to face him. Sheila told him she was glad he had come. She had been very lonely living by herself here. Since she brought the subject up, Joe decided to pursue it. He asked about the evident man who had lived here. She readily admitted that he was her husband. Then she said simply that he was gone now. This seemed all she wanted to say on the matter, so Joe respected her silence and asked no further. The revelation that the man was gone was quite sufficient for him anyway. He dismissed his lingering doubts and they spoke of other things. The subject of the fresh venison came up, and Sheila reminded him that she had promised to be appreciative. The remark disturbed him momentarily. It was almost as if she were implying that her charms had been a form of payment. He instantly regretted having thought it and forced the idea out of his mind. But still, some remnant remained to annoy him.

When they got up, Sheila indicated that she would cook meat that night. She told him that hunters needed to eat well to keep up their strength. Then she jokingly added that lovers had the same requirements. Joe said he would come back later to join her.

When he left the house, Joe looked for his deerskin. It was time to clean and cure it and it was not where he had left it. Fall would not last much longer, and when the first cold blasts heralded winter's approach, he wanted to meet them in buckskin. Alongside a small tool shed, he located the bloody skin and the skinny dog. Wolflike, the undernourished creature had chewed the pelt from end to end. It was now ripped in shreds and quite unusable for the making of clothing.

The bitch saw the man approach and recognized him as the one who had given her a meal; but she was taking no chances. The hand that gave food could as easily take it away. She crouched low over the skin, and growled deep in her throat. She seemed less to be warning Joe off than pleading with him to make fighting unnecessary. This was the food that could fatten her body, and through it, give strength to the little lives within her. She wanted no fight, but for the sake of her babies she would surely defend the food. Joe looked and understood her. She would keep the meal. He thought he would feel the same way if he had children to protect. Joe, thereafter, made a point of bringing the dog some food each time he visited his Sheila.

As he walked toward his shelter, Joe thought about the dog. It seemed a very intelligent creature, but there was about it a certain savage quality that interested him. It had a wildness in its eyes and a way of making its back hairs stand on end that sent a chill through him. If ever there was a thing that had a color that defied description, the dog was it. She was a uniform shade of some blend containing black, gray, brown, and something else. As nearly as he could call it, she was the color of coal mine mud. Her eyes were different, though. There, anything described as common would be totally untrue. The eyes were a brilliant, almost glowing, shade of yellow. Each pupil was a point of jet black. He could tell that the dog had not been treated well. It limped on one hind leg, and the injury appeared to be an old one. She had several scars on her head and body that showed even through the thick coat that was growing in for winter. The dog gave the appearance of being totally beaten. Her carriage and actions spoke of fear, but when her eyes caught the light, they gleamed with a ferocious character. Joe decided that whoever had conquered the dog's body had never managed to subdue her spirit. From those eyes, a fierce freedom still glared. The man wondered idly if the poor old dog might be part wolf.

Joe arrived at his hut and made a few motions toward cleaning things up. During the last few days he had paid little attention to the details of caring for his own wintering spot. He gathered firewood and placed it conveniently near the entrance. When he came back later tonight, thought Joe, at least the campfire could be quickly made. He spread out the bearskin and made his bed ready. Then he checked the one deerskin that he still had. It was in good condition. He would have trousers at least, if not a new jacket. Joe smiled at the memory of the dog crouching to protect the meat-covered skin. The cloth coat from his mining years would have to serve for another season, unless he could find a third deer downriver in the near future.

A hunger was starting to make him think about the cabin. Soon, the prospect of a meal and closeness to the woman pushed Joe off toward the path between the fruit trees. When he left, he carried a long, narrow strip of dried deer meat from his earlier kill. Something about the dog's eyes had made him remember to bring it for her. As he walked, Joe took notice of the subtle changes in the trees. Where only days earlier, green had cloaked them, now they had taken on a blend of red and yellow. The summer was ended. Soon, he knew, he would wake one morning and find the first thin rind of ice on the lagoon. It would be gone by the time the morning sun rose to warm it, but then one day it would stay. It would thicken day by day and all creatures would feel the icy breath of Ya-O-Gah, the north wind. But not yet, thought the Indian, there is still time to gather nuts and other supplies. There is still time to swim and wash. At this thought, he smiled to himself.

He passed through trees and into the cleared, former farm-land. He expected to hear the dog bark and listened for it. There was no bark. He looked toward the dog's usual spots, but each was empty. Still holding the meat, he proceeded to the tool shed. One door was off its rusted hinge, and through the space where it leaned crookedly, Joe saw a paw protruding. When she heard him approach, the female pulled in her exposed foot and snarled out. The sound no longer held any pleading note; it was all warning now. Joe slowly extended the meat, but she still growled menacingly. He tried to push it through to her, but she took this as an aggressive movement. Joe dropped the meat and pulled his hand back in just the nick of time. Her rather impressive teeth came together where his fingers had been a split second earlier. It happened so fast that Joe wasn't sure she had missed. But then she caught the food scent and pulled his offering inside the shed.

While her mouth was occupied with the deer meat, the growling stopped and Joe heard a strange new noise behind the door. It was a wet mewing, so faint that he wasn't sure he heard it. The plaintive little notes kept on though, and soon Joe understood. The puppies had come at last! The Indian felt a powerful urge to see and touch the tiny new lives. But the mother wouldn't allow him any closer than the opening to her lair. She knew and was thankful that he had brought meat for her young, but to allow him near the puppies would violate some instinct stronger than that. Even if she wanted to let him come in, something from her heritage would not have let her do so. If he attempted to enter, she would do her best to kill him. The

primal part of Joe knew all this without his even realizing, and
he kept his distance. She relented to a small degree and finally
let him look in through the opening. The low growl and gleaming yellow eyes put strict limits on his closeness. Joe leaned
only as far as the female permitted and saw the tiny pups
against her body. They were pink and blind and they pushed
weakly at each other for a favorable position against the mother's belly. There were five. She seemed to relax as Joe pulled
back, and when he walked away, the yellow eyes took on an
almost friendly look and followed him until he was out of sight.

Joe mounted the few steps and crossed to the door, but as he
reached to knock, the girl opened it. She had seen him from the
single window. Sheila greeted him with a warm smile, but no
further acknowledgment of the afternoon's passion. A pleasant
smell of cooking venison pushed past her, and Joe was hungry.
He wanted to go in, but she stopped him. Water from the well
was needed and then would he mind picking some of the corn
that stood ripe in her garden patch? She said that even though
there wasn't enough daylight left, he could finish picking it the
next day. Joe felt some sense of rebuff. He had thought the
meeting would somehow be different. Wonderful things had
passed between them only hours earlier. Had she forgotten?
No, that wasn't even possible. He acceded as gracefully as he
could, and set about the farm tasks.

First, Joe drew and carried several buckets of well water. He
poured these into pots and filled the kitchen sink with the rest.
Then he started removing corn from tall stalks and placing it in
wicker bushels. The work was not unpleasant. He was reminded of jobs he had done on many other farms in return for
meals. Joe picked his way back across the autumns of many
years. The golden ears felt familiar to his hands. He could almost see a small Indian boy doing similar work in the long ago,
flanked by a father and mother. Quite without warning, he was
suddenly thinking of the mud-colored dog. He experienced a
rush of emotional hope for her and her babies. The sentimental
thoughts embarrassed him, and he worked harder to block
them out. Before the creeping shadows gave up to the dark of
early evening, Joe had picked many baskets of corn. He himself
was surprised when he looked at the results of his work. It was

small wonder that Sheila expressed her pleasure when she came out to get him.

Sheila held Joe warmly and appreciatively as they walked into the house. The work had been worth the time. Her table was a wonderful sight for hungry eyes to feast upon. The two ate heartily of the venison and various side dishes. Later, with full stomachs, the pair sat and talked. Now and again Joe would stop and look into her eyes. She found it flattering and said nothing to discourage his obvious adoration. The conversation stayed light; she kept it so. But she somehow managed to remind him about the rest of the corn; and again there hovered the suggestion of her appreciation. Joe knew he would pick more the next day. Looking into the blue eyes made the idea not at all distasteful.

Joe mentioned the dog and its new puppies. Sheila smiled. The Indian asked her about the wounds he had seen on the animal. She said that the dog had come one winter and simply refused to leave. It had slept on the porch and foraged its own food. Her husband had taken an instant dislike to the animal and treated it very badly. He frequently hit or kicked it, but still the dog stayed on. Sheila admitted that she had sneaked food to the poor creature on more than one occasion. A day came when her husband kicked the dog and it didn't retreat from him. Two fingers were badly torn on his left hand. After that he had taken an axe and hit the animal. The wound eventually healed, but the limp Joe had seen was permanent. Sheila had no idea about the sire of its pups. Meat had always been a problem here, so she had not been able to feed the animal well. The dog wandered free much of the time hunting for itself. The bitch had never been given a name. Whenever Sheila called it or spoke to it, she addressed it simply as "dog." This told Joe little about the mud-colored animal who suckled her pups in the tool shed, but Sheila knew nothing else. The subject died out and the talk went to other matters. They spoke about swimming, hunting, and the needs of Sheila's farm. The minutes passed into hours, and those fled into the past. Joe saw that Sheila was subtly indicating the evening's end. He had hoped she might ask him to stay, but apparently that was not going to happen. She was warmth and smiles as Joe left. She hoped he would finish with the corn early, said Sheila, so they would have plenty of time tomorrow for other things.

Joe left the house with mixed feelings. He had hoped the evening would prove more exciting. He wondered whether he might have said or done something wrong. Those thoughts evaporated as he neared the tool shed. The chilly light of a fall moon stabbed obliquely through the space where the door hung askew. Through the space shone twin pools of reflected brilliance. The mother dog was watching him. Two Trees stopped to look at the glowing eyes and veered toward them. She didn't growl as he came nearer. The eyes followed his progress until he stood before her. Encouraged, he reached forward. The snarl came, and its message was unmistakable. It said, "I recognize you as the giver of food, but do not threaten my young. That, I cannot allow." Joe drew back. He listened to the mewings from inside. They seemed stronger, more individual now. He smiled.

The autumn days led into Indian summer. One day Joe would find his heart's desires answered; the next they would go unfulfilled. He learned to do Sheila's bidding. The rewards were sometimes worth the work. Somehow though, the intimacy of her bed never seemed to bring them together in more than a bodily manner. It bothered Joe, but he told himself that more would come. He knew the time would arrive when Sheila would give herself in other than physical ways.

During those days an odd thing happened. Each time he went to the farm, Joe brought some meat for the yellow-eyed dog. Once it would be deer meat. Another time it was rabbit. He even brought her smoked fish on occasion, but only when the hunting had been poor. The dog accepted each gift as enthusiastically as the others. She seemed indifferent to the kind of food. She had four pups to feed. One had died soon after birth. The four survivors were hard to satisfy, and she looked forward to Joe's daily visit. There was no growl, no snarl. Now she only placed her body in his way whenever Joe reached to pet her small brood. At last, the day came when she permitted him to touch the furry pups. Only that, though, at first. Gradually she allowed more familiarity, and when they were a few weeks old, Joe was permitted to pick them up. That day he held each for a moment, and in turn, stroked its smooth fur. The female stood at his elbow and gave warning sounds, but she suffered the man, against her instincts, to handle her babies. They were weak and clumsy, small and happy. Each squirmed in the palm of his hand as if demanding he scratch its belly. Joe obliged the little dogs daily. Soon the female took her tiny tribe out of the shed for short stays. First she shooed them into the old lair whenever the Indian approached, but she would remain and meet him. The female developed the habit of licking his hand in thanks for the regular gifts. Eventually she looked forward to his coming, not for the food, but for something else. Gift or no, she now ran to him and licked his hand. The man was kind, gentle. He brought her no pain and her young no danger.

One day, one of the pups ran with the mother to meet Joe. It was a woolly, jet black animal with only one marking. From the base of its nose to the back of its head ran a blaze of white fur. It was a tiny female. Although her coat and color were inherited from some distant ancestor or missing father, heredity had given her the piercing, yellow eyes of the mother.

The frosts of early winter found the dogs learning to forage for themselves. Joe still brought gifts, but it was not easy for him. He set more rabbit snares than the land could really be expected to fill. The little pup with yellow eyes had taken to following Joe wherever he went. Her mother, though, seemed ill. She seldom left the cottage porch anymore. A time came when Joe was unable to fill the meat needs of Sheila, the mother dog, and her pups, not to mention himself. The pups, all but one, left. They struck out on their own to become wild, wolf dogs, or perhaps find a farm where they would be fed and kept. The mother became weaker, day by day, until finally she didn't wake up from one of her ever longer naps. Only the black pup with her yellow eyes stayed on. She stayed by Joe's side, day and night. The growing animal hunted with him, slept with him, and guarded any door that might be closed to shut her off from him.

The red-haired woman presented other problems to Joe. The time of swimming had passed with the cold winds and flying snow. Now he longed to see her naked body, but the opportunities came less often. During the cold time, he came daily from his own place to do various jobs for her, and sometimes he was rewarded. It was not as it had been though. Once she walked to the town past the northern hills and returned late at night with a letter. Joe saw her look at the talking words and smile. She refused, though, to tell him their message. As was normal with a farm, little work remained to be done during this season. He did his best to make himself valuable to her, but it was difficult. He began to understand that her interest in him was proportional to her need for his services. To offset the lack of farm work, Joe spent more time hunting. Often he would be gone for days. The dog was always with him. She shared in his kills, and she proved to be a strong and able hunter. Sometimes, she would come to Joe with a rabbit, and then the man would share the dog's kill.

It was often during those nights on the trail that the young dog would spontaneously come to his side, look up and lick his hand. When she did, he would see the glowing eyes and marvel at the similarity to those of her dead mother. When he made an improvised camp and stopped to sleep, the dog's warmth was dependable and welcome. Joe never mistreated the animal, and even when the hunting brought them no meat, she seemed satisfied to nourish herself on his kindness.

The dog ate well and thrived. She grew, before spring, into a formidable beast. Sometimes Joe would stop what he was doing just to look at her. It amazed him. The dog hadn't completed one full season of life yet, but her size was already astounding. At some dim point in the animal's evolution, traits of a large bone structure and leonine head had been genetically planted. When she put her forepaws on his shoulders in affectionate play, the Indian was very glad that she only wanted to lick his face.

As she developed, the dog began to show other singular traits. Joe was hers, and she watched over him jealously. If any animal, domestic or wild, squirrel or bear, presented itself, she assumed that it threatened her master. No creature was allowed to approach him. This proved to be an inconvenience at times, even a downright danger. The dog could easily attack and kill a creature the size of a pig. Since Joe worked with Sheila's few farm animals, he taught the dog that they must be left alone. She learned quickly and understood the lesson, but whenever he walked among those animals, she crouched nearby, growling her warning to them. Joe would pat her and say reassuring words, but her vigilance remained constant.

As much as the dog was growing to love Two Trees, she came to dislike Sheila. The enmity sometimes seemed to border on open hatred. Nothing that Joe could do or say seemed to alleviate the situation. Where the dog had aloofly permitted Sheila to pet her as a puppy, now she forbade it. The eyes and the rumbling growl told Sheila to keep her distance. Was it simple jealousy or some mystic sense dogs are sometimes said to possess? They say it is good judgment to beware of the person disliked by a dog.

The winter passed slowly. Joe hunted and filled in time by doing repairs and chores at the farm. He provided meat and worked at his hunting with a passion. He imagined that the flesh he brought might revive Sheila's old appreciation, but the more he did, the less she seemed to notice. With her stomach kept full and sufficient meat stored away, she grew indifferent to his kills.

Then the easing weather told Joe that planting time was approaching, and he asked Sheila if she had seed for the fields. There was some, but not enough. That night in his wigwam, Joe searched through his pouch. There were still several silver dollars he had managed to retrieve from the snow that winter long ago. These had rested, unneeded and unused, for all the time since. As Joe looked at the money in the wavering firelight, he smiled and thought back across the intervening years. There had been Tony, the homeless rabbit, the great bear. Then Cass had crossed the path of his life. After Cass there had come Sheila and now the powerful dog, so much a part of Joe's existence. As he thought this, the Indian wondered why he had unconsciously grouped the red-haired woman with the others that were now a part of his past. Why had his mind relegated all those to the time that had been, while keeping only the dog in the present, and time yet to come? But then he discarded the thought and thanked his Great Spirit for all of them. Each in his or her own way had made his life better, his trail easier. The Great Spirit, thought Joe, must surely still love Two Trees to have given him all these.

Early in the morning, the Indian brought the few dollars to Sheila. He told her to go to the village and buy seed. While she was gone, he would clean the rusted plow and pull it through the hardened furrows, preparing the ground. She agreed readily, and soon was gone.

Joe worked at the weedy soil, using his back to replace the horse or mule lacking on this farm. The work was hard, but Joe didn't mind it. This was good work, tied to soil and growing things. It was a far cry from the labor of mining that had hardened his muscles, but left his soul unfulfilled. As he went, the dog was ever at his side. Her job was a self-appointed one; to guard him. This she did, up one plowed row and down the next, all through the day. Sometimes, Joe would stop to rest and pet the dog. When he did, her wagging tail showed that the wait had been a worthwhile one for her.

When the darkness began to fall, Joe stopped plowing. Sheila hadn't returned yet. He sat on the steps, watching for her in the direction she had gone. When it was too dark to continue the vigil, Joe began to worry. He walked to the wigwam and brought his bearskin back to Sheila's porch. There, with his dog, Joe spent the night, waiting. It was damp and cold, but he never thought to go inside. That might make him miss some sound or sign of her approach. The night was long, and she did not appear. At first light he could take no more of the inactivity. Two Trees set out to follow her trail toward the settlement.

The tracking was easy for the Indian, even though Sheila's trail was now a day old. It required concentration though, since she could have taken any number of routes. A footprint in soft ground, a bent twig, or a thread trapped by some wayside thorn bush all pointed him in the right direction. But these detections slowed him down, and it was already late afternoon when he stood looking down at the cluster of houses. He circled in an arc, to intercept any trail she might have made by leaving by a different route, but there was none. Sheila was still in town. The dog at his side began to snarl at the nearness of the houses, and Joe had to hush her. He settled into the brush to watch the houses for some sign of the woman. The dog stretched out by his side to wait with him.

There she was. Joe caught sight of her unmistakable hair as she came out the door of one of the houses. A man followed close behind and put one arm around her waist. As Joe watched, they exchanged a few words. When she turned to leave, he patted her quite intimately on her rounded behind. Hot anger rose in the Indian, and sensing it, his dog bristled darkly. But the woman made no objection. She turned and smiled at the man instead. Joe held the dog, who had also seen Sheila and now snarled in her direction fiercely. Joe watched as the woman entered the woods to his left. She carried a rolled paper and two packages. He hid for a few moments, not wanting her to know he had followed. When she was out of sight, he started at a trot along a different path back to the farm. He wanted to be there, plowing, when she returned, and he was.

When Sheila arrived, he made no mention of her overnight absence, and she remained just as silent about it. Joe noticed that the rolled paper was a newspaper. He knew of those as talking-word carriers of things that had happened in other, sometimes distant, places. It did not impress him anymore that the whites could hear talk from words on paper. He just accepted it as a fact that would always be beyond him.

One of Sheila's packages contained seeds, but he could see at a glance they were not sufficient to plant even the portion of land he already had prepared, so he stopped work. The other package held an amber bottle. Two Trees knew that it was whiskey. He knew of its dubious powers, even though he had never tasted it.

15

The Yellow-Eyed Dog

As Joe was putting the farm implements away in the shed, his dog began to growl. Joe could see nothing that would have bothered her, but he had learned to trust her senses more than his own. She turned toward the tree line and stood stiffly, sniffing the breeze. Soon, her back hairs bristled from head to tail. With a terrible snarl, she shot away and across the plowed field, disappearing into the trees. Joe ran after her.

Suddenly he heard awful barks and snarls, mixed with high-pitched screams of pain. Two Trees first thought that the dog had scented some animal stalking the livestock. Perhaps a bear or a wildcat had come to raid the farm. He worried for the dog and grabbed a heavy branch to use as a club. When he reached the scene of the fighting, Joe saw that the dog needed no help from him. She had the quarry bloodied and down. It was not an animal; it was a man. Joe called the dog, but she was out of his control. She was bent on killing the man. Then Joe saw why. She had a deep gash over one eye where the stranger must have hit her with something. A few feet off, Joe saw the object. It was a long-barreled revolver. Blood clung wet and red, mixed with black hairs, to its length. Joe picked up the gun and fired it into the air. At the sharp blast, the dog jumped back and Joe grabbed her by the back of the neck. He held her and soothed her with calm words until the blood lust had gone from her eyes. Meanwhile, the stranger rolled himself away and propped his back against the trunk of a tree. He sat there, dazed and bleeding, watching the animal dumbly. When Joe was sure he had regained authority over the excited animal, he slowly let her go. She stood, glaring and growling, between her master and the man.

Joe rose and tucked the gun into his waistband. The badly frightened man made no objection. Joe walked forward to examine the man's wounds. He still sat, speechless. He had several small tears, but most were not serious. The man's heavy winter clothing had absorbed much of the dog's fury. His right hand was more deeply bitten than any other place. The dog had apparently grabbed it in order to disarm the man. He was silently glad she had bitten that hand that had hurt her. Joe said nothing, but motioned for the man to rise. He did this, but with obvious pain. Joe pointed toward the clearing. He wanted to examine this man who stole silently upon isolated farms. Hunters carried rifles, or shotguns, not pistols. Joe wanted him in the clear, away from the shadowy trees. He advised the stranger that only one word would bring the dog to the man's throat.

In the plowed field, Joe looked the intruder over. He wore boots that had seen many roads. They were worn and thin. The rest of his clothing was torn and dirty. Some rips were new, made by the dog, but most were not. They spoke of much travel. His jacket, which might once have been blue, was fastened with a row of brass buttons.

Joe demanded to know why the man had been hidden among the trees. With a quick look toward the dog, the man answered, honestly, that he had hoped to steal a chicken for food. He had probably decided the truth might go better on him than the possible consequences of any lie. Joe nodded, he could understand such a motive as hunger. The man said he was a farmer, but had most recently been a soldier. He told Joe enough for the Indian to know that he had been fighting in the war that was going on—the war that Cass had gone to join. There, he had been badly wounded and then taken captive by his enemies. The man pulled aside the ripped leg of his trousers and pointed, as if offering proof of his story. Most of the calf muscle had been ripped away and was only newly covered with poorly healed scar tissue. Joe understood then that the man's limp had not been caused entirely by his dog. The limp would accompany him for the balance of his life, but only if he was lucky enough to keep the mutilated leg at all.

The Indian realized that this man was more to be pitied than feared. He was so weak that he would be able to offer no threat even if he wanted to try. The dog also seemed to have sensed this. She had done her job of protecting the master, and now that she believed there was no further danger, she ignored the man. But even as she disregarded him, she remained alert to all possibilities. She would let him live, but only as long as the master wanted it.

Joe invited him to the farm for food and rest, but kept the pistol, not ready to give its power back to an unknown man. When they reached the house, Sheila stood on the porch watching them. Joe briefly explained the circumstances and she showed concern for the man's cuts. He asked if there was a place nearby where he could wash. Joe pointed toward the river, telling the man that although the water was still cold, it was clean. The stranger smiled for the first time and said it would do fine. Then Sheila asked if he would care for her to come and wash his wounds. The man's second smile was abruptly halted by the jarring order Joe gave her. "Inside." He said only the one word, but its tone and intensity carried volumes of meaning. It was enough to set the dog's hair bristling again, and Sheila scurrying through the door. There was anger in the Indian, but it was not for the poor chicken thief.

Joe went to the river and helped the man for a few moments, but his main concern was for the dog. He gently bathed her wound. The dog understood his good intentions, and she stood still in the cold water while he washed dirt from the bloody scalp. The touches must have brought some pain, but she never flinched. The hand of her master was always welcome. The three completed their wash and walked back to the farm. Even though the man still stole nervous glances at the black dog with its slightly reddened mark of white, Joe could tell she no longer was angry. That the dog seemed unperturbed went a long way toward settling any lingering doubts about the former soldier. Joe asked him to tell more about his captivity. It had been very short. The captors had expected him to die and had not watched him carefully. One night, he got up and simply limped out of their camp. Probably thinking he would soon die in the wilderness, they had not bothered to follow him. He fooled them and did not die. But he decided that he wanted no more war. Avoiding contact with friendly troops and enemy alike, he slowly made his way north. The stranger was heading for Albany. There, he had been a farmer, but that was almost two years earlier.

Joe was sorry for the man and silently decided to give him food for the rest of his journey. A meal and a place to rest for a day were all that would be added to the food, however. He had learned, years ago, that one who gets overly involved in the problems of others would neglect his own needs. Joe would send this man on his way the next day, toward whatever was ultimately to be his fate.

When the old Indian told me this part of his story, I was not quite sure if I detected some small note of jealousy. If it was actually jealousy for the dwindling romance with Sheila, I don't think Two Trees was even aware of it. He simply wanted the man gone, so he would not have to add him as a factor to contend with in his formula for survival. Also, then he could give back the pistol and be rid of it. It was not a conscious matter of distrust, but even though the dog seemed satisfied, the man had sneaked up on them once before.

Joe took the gun from his waist and studied it. It looked to be a very efficient weapon. Trusting the stranger was one thing, but risking the lead from his pistol was entirely another. Joe released the cylinder and emptied its remaining cartridges into his hand. He looked at them for a moment and then toward the house. No one was in sight. He reached back and threw the bullets as far away as he could. The dog watched silently as they fell among the leaves and were lost.

He scratched her gently behind the ears, careful to avoid the long, matted gash, and her tail waved approval. She stayed close to his leg as they walked to the house. When he entered, the man and Sheila were closely examining the newspaper. It was spread open on the table, and they were both hunched over it, speaking of places he had never heard about. Then he saw that the whiskey bottle stood open between them. The two had ignored him until then, but Sheila noticed his irritation and offered him a drink. To be included, he accepted. She fetched a glass and poured a quantity for him. Joe picked it up and sniffed. Then he noticed that they were both watching him with an air of expectation. Self-consciously, he hefted the glass to his mouth and downed it at a gulp. First his eyes watered, then his throat began to burn, and finally he was taken over by a fit of coughing. The two laughed at him until tears ran from their eyes. It had been a great joke to everyone except Joe. He rose and silently left the house.

He walked in darkness, accompanied by yellow-eyes until, eventually, his anger and resentment ebbed. The warming breeze of a spring evening soothed and calmed him. Joe forced himself to see the whiskey incident as a harmless prank, and as he walked to the cabin, he almost believed it. Joe went back inside, trying very hard to smile. The effort was wasted on the other two. Much of the whiskey was gone, and they disregarded Two Trees's return. They were laughing and talking, giving the appearance of two very old friends, rather than people who had met only earlier that same day. They were still talking about the war, and Sheila seemed pleased to hear the man's view that the North would soon be victorious. Joe, in no way concerned about the war's outcome, was nonetheless interested in Sheila's reactions. During all the time Two Trees had known her, she had never even mentioned the war.

The friendly pair finally remembered Joe's presence, and the man asked if he was an Indian. Joe guardedly admitted that he was. He sensed or expected trouble over this, but the other only smiled and nodded. The Indian was glad it had not come to more, but still he was anxious to be done with this soldier. The sooner he was gone, the better Joe would feel about the whole matter. The Indian inquired if the stranger planned to leave early the next day. The affirmative response encouraged him, and he took the revolver out. He told the stranger he would give it back now to save him time in the morning.

Joe placed it on the table, and the man took it. In the same motion he rose and spun toward the door where the dog lay watching. He aimed and pulled the trigger, but the hollow click of an empty chamber sounded almost simultaneously with the grinding crunch of strong teeth meeting bone. The dog had launched herself as soon as he began to turn. The sight of that hated metal club had been all the impetus needed to turn her into a raging beast. She grabbed his hand, disarming him as she had earlier in the trees. There was a difference though. This time she would not release her grip. Her large, black body pinned the former soldier across the chest as she gnawed at his hand. The sound of splintering bone was unmistakable.

The man screamed in fear and pain, but Joe only looked on. The woman was horrified and unable even to scream. She watched the growing pool of blood, then suddenly turned and ran behind the curtain of blankets. Slowly, Joe picked up the pistol; for want of any better way to destroy it, he dropped the weapon into the hearth fire.

Joe stood in front of the fire, deliberately watching the gun's wooden hand grips char and burst into flame. When he judged that the dog had spent sufficient time exacting her revenge, he turned to her and called softly. She either didn't hear or chose to disregard him. At last he had to pull her roughly away from the slobbering man. Joe absently noticed two indisputable facts. The broad, red stain would never be fully removed from the plank floor, and the limping farmer would never again find any serious use for his right hand. Two Trees held his dog and allowed the man to rise on wobbly feet. He staggered, and for a moment Joe thought he might be physically unable to leave. Then the man straightened and looked fearfully toward the door. The Indian told him to go and he added that he would soon release the dog to follow him. Although he hadn't any intention of doing so, the soldier had no way of knowing it. The last that Joe saw of him was his stumbling silhouette retreating into the darkness. Somehow, Joe was very sure they had seen the last of the wounded deserter.

Some time elapsed while Two Trees sat at the table, with the big animal's head resting across his lap. He crooned to her, soothing back the killer part that showed visibly through her brilliant eyes. The dog had forgiven her hurt once, but when the stranger threatened her a second time, he had committed an unpardonable act. In all the world, she wanted but one thing at that moment. She wanted to hunt. She wanted to follow the hated man relentlessly, across forest and field and overtake him. As Joe ran his hands across her broad back, he could feel the rigid musculature, tensed for combat. The pleading look she gave him told all he wanted to know. Two Trees shuddered. He had no wish to see the man killed. He had only wanted him gone, and that he surely was.

It was quite late when Sheila came back into the room. She was white, to a frightening degree, and tear stains marked her face. She walked past Joe, giving both him and the dog a very wide berth. The partly filled bottle still stood where it had been. She sat down across from him and lifted it to her lips. Joe watched, amazed that she could tolerate the burning fluid. The level grew lower and lower as it emptied down her throat. She seemed to be trying hard, with eyes forced shut, to close out the bloody mess around her and the vivid horror within. When she put the bottle down, the whiskey was nearly gone.

Still holding her eyes shut, Sheila spoke to Joe. The cold hatred in her voice was evident with the first syllable. The dog was calm by that time, but the sound of that voice brought her hairs up and a growl to her throat. At the same time, Joe recognized in Sheila's voice some quality that told him he had been a fool. No wife, no mother, no loving partner, could this woman ever be.

She told Joe, as sarcastically as she could, that he and his horrible dog were both animals as far as she was concerned. She told him he should forget about trying to wear clothing like a man; he should run naked in the woods with the filthy bitch, attacking decent white people as they went. He was not fit company for human beings. She cried that Joe had managed to run off the only white man to visit her since her husband left for the army. "But," she added, "I hope you stay around here. When my husband does return, I will see that he kills you and your bitch." Joe rose and calmly said that he would take her advice about staying with the dog, then he would know he was in better company than now.

As he left he knew there would be nothing further between them, but he realized too, that there had been little from the start. She had needed meat and farm work, and had paid for them. He wasn't angry at her. He had given, and he had gotten in return. If he had been foolish enough to believe she saw more in him than what he was, her parting speech about "decent white people" showed him that the error had been his.

Joe knew it was much better this way. He was, again, a free

being. Now he even had the great, black guardian. He was not angry, and he tried not to feel hurt. For the most part, he was successful, but still, there had been the hope.

As Joe told me the part of his story that included Sheila, I was too young to fully understand. Yet, in my later years I would remember it all. And I would also remember that although he had insisted it was really unimportant, he contradicted himself by spending more time on Sheila's story, and recalling more details, than on any other. While he told it, I could feel that I'd become a part of each scene. His description of cloud colors and passing seasons were so vivid, I often sensed he was living it again through the telling. Even as he spun a web of cruelty and promiscuity, in which the girl's character was inexorably trapped, he hastened, periodically, to defend her. "It was not really her fault. How could she have been otherwise?" he said more than once.

Joe was a human being who saw goodness in beauty, and beauty in nature. The woman was beauty to his eyes, and so she was naturally good. This, with him, was not rationalization, but instinct. I suggest, much over the protestations of a long-dead Indian, that Joe loved her very much. He loved her for the physical, the emotional, and for the deeply seated hope that somehow he would not be the last of his line. Yes, I think that even as he damned her, Joe loved her still. I believe that the little campfire at Hunter Island burned brighter for him as he told of the girl, and it was joined by a flame in his heart that had never quite gone out. There is a last fact. Joe never tried again to establish any relationship with another woman.

He left her that night and only saw her once again. That once was from a distance. He more than left. Joe removed himself from her. The distance that separated them could have been as broad as the gulf between the stars, but it was, in actuality, only as far as his wigwam. The Indian spent several days near the home, thinking of his next journey. He wasn't upset by Sheila's threat about her husband. During the winter he had strongly suspected that there was such a person anyhow. Joe now knew of the dog's abilities and her strong urge to protect him, so he was sure no man could sneak up undetected. The years had also taught him to rely on his strength and cunning. Together, thought Joe, they were a match for any man.

16

A Dugout Canoe

He began to make preparations and gather provisions for a trip.
Joe had decided to be done with this side of the river. Now,
when he was ready, he would cross it in a dugout canoe. The
canoe would be like the one he had made with his father, in the
long ago. He slept that night with happy dreams. A small boy
trotted along with his tall father, doing wonderful things. They
hunted and fished, farmed and gathered. The father showed his
son the correct making of a dugout canoe. A red-haired woman
ran across his field of view, and the dream ended with the small
boy crying, lost, looking for his father. Joe woke then, and
vividly remembered those images. He thought for a moment
and decided that despite the crying, it had been a happy dream.
It was good to have looked at his father's face again. Then he
felt the close warmth of his dog and dropped back into peaceful, undisturbed sleep. He woke to a new world. Birds sang in
the sunshine, underscored by the muted surge of the river.

Two Trees, very much the Indian again, needed an Indian
making to undertake. It would occupy his hands and his mind,
and in proper Algonquin fashion, even his heart. He remembered a straight, thick tulip tree that stood near the river, a bit
downstream. Joe gathered his things from the winter shelter
and walked the short distance to the tree. That tree was to
become *mushoon,* his father's word for the dugout canoe. It
disturbed Joe slightly that he had needed to think for a moment
to remember the word. As he looked the tree over, gauging and

judging it for his purpose, Two Trees tried to remember other words from the speech of his boyhood. Joe wanted to remember. It was now an important thing to become again as he had once been. He had not spoken the native tongue to any living person since the death of his mother, and through disuse, it had faded to a large degree. Even his thoughts came up to his conscious mind in a poor combination of Algonquin concepts put to white man's words. He discovered, though, that by concentrating very hard, he could still remember quite a lot. If he closed his eyes, Joe could easily hear in his mind the tone and inflection in Eagle Feather's voice as he had spoken the sometimes guttural, often musical phrases of daily life. It hurt him to admit that some of the actual words were blurred and lost in time.

The ever-present dog looked happily up from her position at his feet. Joe noticed the broad shoulders and powerful legs, and a thought came to mind. In all creation, the Maker's wonders had names. Man and woman had special names so they could be told apart from others of their kind. Certainly such a wonderful creature as the great, black dog deserved a distinctive name. He had given it no thought, until now, probably because it was seldom necessary to call the animal, since it almost lived in the Indian's shadow. But now it was time. The animal must have a fine, fearsome name. And it would be an Indian name.

He examined the dog closely and considered her many attributes, hoping one of these would suggest the name. But the forgotten language hampered him. Finally, with some sense of frustration, he settled on the only name that seemed at all appropriate. It was *Mekane*. In the old times he had known that word. It meant, simply, dog. Eventually, through usage and ease of speech, Mekane would come to be said as only "Kane." Gradually she understood and came to love the sound of her name from Joe's lips.

Not far from the tulip tree, Two Trees set up a temporary lean-to shelter. It would not be needed for an entire season. If Great Spirit smiled upon his project, it would be needed only for days, at most, weeks. Joe gathered plenty of wood and piled it near the base of his chosen tree. He ringed the base with a circular fire and began to burn the trunk through. As the wood charred, he chipped and chopped away to expose fresh wood for the flames. This took longer than he had anticipated, but after several days he was rewarded by a splintering sound. The narrow base had, at last, become too thin to support the heavy tree. Down it came with a heavy thud and Joe had accomplished the first part of his making.

With the trunk now lying on the ground, Joe measured off the proper length. At that point he built another fire on both sides and over the fallen tree. It might not have been as efficient as a large saw, but it would serve. This job was to be done in the Indian way. More than anything about the mushoon, Two Trees wanted it to be Indian. He tended the fire and watched his tree slowly develop the shape he wanted under the eroding flames. The progress was gradual, but sure. He was happy. The work was good to have. It gave him purpose again, and that was a valued thing.

Joe remembered the stone tools he had used when he last did this thing. There had been an axe to help the flames remove wood and an adze to gouge away the char. These were a part of the making; he would make them, too. Two Trees couldn't recall exactly how his father had fashioned these tools, but he had a good mental image of the way they worked and what they looked like. That would be enough. All he needed were stone and time. Those commodities presented no problems to Joe Two Trees. A short walk along the pebble beach provided plenty of stone blanks having the right general shape for his tools. He took several and sat down on a flat rock to examine them. One was hard and had a flattened, round shape. It became his hammer stone. Another was heavy and elongated. It tapered, more narrow at one end than the other. It required fairly little striking to bring the narrow end to a rough blade. Joe considered the need for a handle and decided he would use it in a handheld fashion unless one were required later. Even then, it would not be hard to peck a groove around its top and attach a handle with strips of rawhide. For now, though, the axe was finished.

The Indian looked through his stock of blanks for a rock to use for the adze. None was quite right. A second walk located more blanks, but still none seemed to lend itself to the proper shaping. Joe began to see that the adze would require more work on his part and less dependence on natural forms. The adze, though basically axelike in form, would need one deeply concaved face, and nature seemed not overly helpful with that distinction. Joe's hands would have to form the concave. He set to it. As he was destined to do many years later, along with a small white boy, he made many "scrapers" that day. The art of flaking out a rounded impression with any depth was not simple for Joe, but after much trial and error he made a passable instrument. Back on the right trail at last, he returned to the tree.

Joe was not surprised to see that the fire had died during his long absence. It was just as well, however. He tested both of the new implements on the narrow, blackened segment that still attached his future boat to its mother tree. The hand axe cut through the remaining wood! Joe was inwardly proud of his efforts. Indian he was, and Indian he would be again—that was his resolve. The spirits of his people were watching, and he had done well in their eyes. He smiled and talked long and impressively to Kane. He told her of the importance of this making and of his heritage. He spoke of the love that it showed the Great Spirit to have for both of them. Kane wagged her bushy tail in excited response, happy in the happiness of her master. But, Joe remembered, his ancestors were now watching for practicality, not exuberance. The time of rejoicing was not yet. That would be more appropriate when the day came that saw Two Trees and Kane afloat.

Chastened somewhat, Joe examined the results of his work thus far. There was still a lot to be done. He now had a log of the proper length, and bluntly rounded at each end, but still only a log. The process of hollowing it into a boat was one to which Two Trees had only given vague thought until then. Now it presented itself in stark reality, as the next required step. He knew that fire was the primary tool for the operation, but controlling it along the top of a rounded log would be difficult. He started to chop out a long cavity with his axe, but soon saw the problems of a handheld instrument. Holding the axe head in his hand did not give enough thrust to make it effective. The axe required a handle after all. Joe accomplished this with no trouble, and he was then able to chop out a long cavity to hold the wood for his fire. Once he started the fire, he found that it was advantageous to keep it small and near the center of the compartment he would eventually occupy. Each time sufficient wood was burnt into charcoal, he would widen the hole with the axe and gouge it lengthwise with the adze. The work went slowly, with the speed of burning being its limiting factor, but each day the log became more and more boatlike in appearance.

Joe's original estimate of how long it would take to make his mushoon proved to have been a bit optimistic, but the end product was well worth the time spent. When the lengthening days of early summer were warming the river into the frenetic life required by a short, northern season, Joe was ready to venture upon it. One afternoon he loaded most of his provisions into the boat and covered them with his bearskin. He walked around the area for one last time, looking, examining. He wanted the details of this particular winter encampment to stay, etched upon the screen of his memory. Many things had happened here; things Joe knew had changed his life to something different than it would otherwise have been. He would leave in the morning, and he would have many mixed feelings at this leaving. But it wasn't morning yet. He still had time to walk and remember.

Joe went to the winter wigwam. This was where he had had the dream of walking at Hunter Island with Eagle Feather. He walked farther north and crouched where he had waited for the smart old buck. He wandered back along the bank to the hidden lagoon. Many memories lingered still among those reeds. A small, involuntary smile crept across his aquiline features. Drawn almost against his will, he walked the familiar path through fruit trees grown lush and verdant.

Joe stopped at the tree line and noticed that Sheila had not bothered to plant the furrows he had so laboriously claimed from the earth. It was growing dark then, and as he watched the house, a lantern was lit inside. Its pale glow showed dimly through the single window. He wondered momentarily how Sheila would survive when winter came. She had planted no crops, and no one would be there to hunt meat for her. Perhaps her husband would return, but perhaps he would not. He forced the thoughts out of his mind. Sheila was not his responsibility, although he had once wished it otherwise.

Through that night, the dog trotted dutifully at his side, but at sight of the farm, Kane had flattened her ears back and started a low rumble in her throat. She relaxed only when her master turned toward the river and the dugout canoe.

They arrived back at the canoe and Joe examined it closely by the dim light of stars and moon. He was pleased with the boat. It had a sleek, neat look about it. Joe had spent time smoothing its hull of splinters, and curving the bow to slice waves and water. He knew that all these details were not strictly necessary for its purpose, but the wood had fascinated him. He found great pleasure in rubbing it with stone and making it good to the touch. Now, when he passed his palm along the craft's flank, its feel delighted him.

The day of leaving finally dawned. It could have been a nasty, drizzling day, with a northeast wind to dampen his spirits. If it had been, he might have procrastinated further. It wasn't, though. This day was born in the womb of a brilliant eastern sky, with the promise of warmth and gentle breeze. Joe was ready. Then he noticed one small detail. In his desire to make a fine boat, he had forgotten to provide a paddle for its propulsion. He wondered bleakly whether the eyes of his ancestors had noticed this small oversight. Joe found suitable wood, and using his flint knife, consumed the morning making the paddle he would need. He wondered at the fact that even when he was finished wasting time, events had conspired to make him use still more. Had he forgotten the paddle, or had he tried to forget it? He wasn't sure. If he had hoped the woman might come to him during this time, she did not.

By midday, he had a paddle, a boat, and all that he wanted, except any further excuse for staying. Joe dragged the canoe to the water's edge and stood, holding it with its stern still aground. Then he indicated, by pointing, that he wanted Kane to climb in. She waded out and sniffed at the bobbing, little shell, not at all sure it looked safe. The master seemed sure, though, so Kane climbed over its side somewhat dubiously. Then Joe pushed out a bit farther and he too entered. His judgment had been good. The boat floated, even loaded as it was, with sufficient freeboard. Joe sat for a few moments, not paddling. He wanted to feel the boat and get to know it. Joe rocked his weight from side to side, and realized the craft's limitations. It would be good practice to keep most of the

weight in the center. Overall, though, the boat seemed as good
on the water as it had on the bank. The craft would serve well,
he decided. He encouraged Kane to lay her bulk down at the
dugout's bottom, but she was interested in this new experience
and kept popping up to see what was going on around her. Joe
managed to time her movements with his own and soon it presented no great problem. He knelt in the bottom and found his
best location for balance. That would be his paddling station.
He was ready.

Joe maneuvered the boat around until its bow pointed toward midriver. Then he dug the paddle in and his strong shoulders gave it force. The sleek boat cut through water and the
bank fell behind rapidly. On the spur of the moment, he turned
to look back at the lagoon.

The powerful current had carried him downstream a bit, but
the relative curvature of the shoreline had placed him in direct
line with the narrow entrance between tall reeds. There, Joe
saw Sheila, swimming. The sight of Joe in his canoe startled
her, and she stood up to watch him pass. He saw the full
breasts again, as he had so many other times. He watched the
way a sunbeam caught the redness of her hair and broke into
sparkles of flame. Then, his eyes met hers. Even at this distance
her own held visible hate, unabated by the separation that had
lasted more than a month.

The current carried him farther and farther away, and only
when Sheila was a speck, lost against the rushes, did Joe dig his
paddle into the mighty flow.

17

On the Hudson River

It was warm. He felt strength flow from the water, through the wood, and into his body. He dipped a hand over the side and splashed water across his chest periodically. It cooled him and washed away his perspiration. He had the dog for company. Fish surfaced here and there, creating swirls of small turbulence with their passing. The boat, mushoon, glided through a river filled with life. If he neared one shore or the other, water lilies, frogs, dragonflies, and muskrats abounded. When he drifted toward the center of the flow, fish came up to puzzle over his passing.

Later, he let the boat drift into some reeds, and stopped to rest. Insects humming and the gentle motion of his dugout soon lulled Two Trees into napping. Now and then he opened his eyes to smile at the dog, but soon she too dozed, so Joe allowed himself to drift deeper into sleep. The afternoon sun was still quite warm on his skin, and it reinforced his sense of well-being. No cares had Joe Two Trees, no worries to disturb his rest. He slept peacefully and for a long time.

Something tugging at his brain forced it back to awareness. He opened his eyes and was surprised to find it nearly dark around him. Kane stood above him, her shadow blocking his light. She was sounding her deep warning growl. The animal had heard some danger and stood over him to guard, with her body, if need should arise. Joe motioned her to be quiet and listened for whatever had brought her to the alert.

First he heard nothing but the normal river and woods sounds. Then he noticed that the birds in nearby trees had stopped singing. The dog had not been mistaken. Danger, or its potential, did lurk somewhere nearby. Finally, Joe heard the voices. They were low, whispered sounds moving with some degree of stealth along the riverbank. The thought occurred to Two Trees that they might be stalking him, until he remembered that no one knew he was here, or even that he existed. He disregarded an impulse that wanted him to grab the paddle and dig into the river. Instead of fleeing, he would stay hidden in the dugout and get a look at these invaders of his privacy. Joe had forced the big dog flat and flattened himself also. The low dugout now appeared, to a casual eye, like any other half-submerged log in the swampy coves along the river. As they passed, he eased one eye over the edge of the boat and studied them. Their equipment and actions told Joe they were hunters. The pair was intent on putting food on the family table, nothing more. The Indian was relieved to know they had not been some more dangerous threat. Their presence, though, forced Joe to confront several ideas that he had not yet faced.

The arrival of the hunters reminded him that somewhere down the river was the large city of New York. He knew he was still far to the north of it, but he had no idea how far. A second thought jolted him. He might be closer to it than he thought! Also, he had no way to know if other large cities lay between here and New York. Of one thing, though, he knew he could be sure. Every day that the river carried him toward her end would bring him closer to the white world, its throngs of alien people, its cities. Joe was not pleased at the prospect. He had avoided whites, with the exception of Sheila, for a long time now. He distrusted them and was certain that he would come out the loser in any meeting. The thought that he would see more of them each day and finally be surrounded by them was frightening to the Indian.

He considered that it might be better to turn the boat's bow north and regain the solitude that lay that way, but he had covered the territory once already. No happy circumstance would be found waiting there. He decided to paddle slowly along the shoreline and find a comfortable spot to stop for the night. There, he would make a fire, eat, and think this matter

over at his leisure. Joe backwatered with his paddle and freed
the canoe from its weedy mooring. He paddled back into the
main flow, and the current's strength made further strokes necessary only to keep the boat on course. Shortly, he saw an ideal
landing spot and directed the boat to it.

He paddled aground on a pleasant little beach. Only one
feature distinguished it from any of the others along the river.
A tall boulder jutted up near the water's edge. Joe decided it
would offer a good perch for watching the activities of fish in
the reeds below. Also, and more practically, it gave him an
excellent vantage point to survey the river in both directions for
some distance. This small margin of safety pleased the wary
Indian. Above the bank grew an extensive bramble of blackberries, and they were ripe. Joe had seen all he wanted to see. This
place would serve very well for a day, or possibly more. He
looked at Kane and noticed that she was happily sniffing at a
rabbit trail among the spiny vines. Joe picked a few berries and
munched as he walked back to unload the dugout.

He laid out his sleeping gear and built a small pile of twigs.
Later, against the chill of evening, he might need a warming
fire. His appetite had been satisfied by the berries, so the fire
would not be needed for cooking food after all. The clear sky
showed good weather for the evening, so he didn't bother to
construct any shelter. The Maker's stars would be roof enough
for this night. Joe picked a few more berries, and then he fed
the dog some dried deer meat. As always, she ate it as much
because the master gave it as to fill her stomach.

Joe walked to the tall rock and looked for a foothold. Finding one, he stepped up and pulled himself to the top. There, a
rounded projection fit perfectly against the small of his back,
and Joe leaned against it. The sun was just starting to drop
behind high bluffs across the water. Joe was impressed with the
rapid change in the river's character. With the disappearance of
sunlight, a silence fell. Birds chirped only occasionally now,
and in softly muted tones. Even the gentle breeze, which had
ruffled the water during the afternoon, had dropped to a
whisper and faded away.

As Joe looked at the passing water, it reminded him of a
disturbing fact. This was a crossroad. If he left this camp and
went back on the river, it would take him to a place he had

already been. So, too, if he turned north. There was no reason he could not endure the stares and glances of white men. He had done it once before, when he first entered their city. But why would he want to? He could visit the city this once to look for Tony. It was a good thought. Joe knew he would be pleased to see that man again after all these years. Then he would leave. The city was not a place for Joe Two Trees, Algonquin.

But when he left—where would he go then? Was it only chance that had brought him in a nearly complete circle? Joe wondered, that with all the world open to him, his feet had slowly measured out a course that finally aimed him toward his starting point. Had he done this on purpose?

He wrestled with the matter for many more days and nights. The short layover stretched into July and then August. Once, he was almost decided that he would strike out toward the east and whatever might lie there. Then, just before he was about to start out, he placed his hand upon the mushoon. Its smooth wood reminded him of the work that had gone to build it. Such a fine boat should not be deserted and left to rot. He didn't go east. He didn't go anywhere.

Something new started to come into his mind on occasion. It wasn't really new. More accurately it was old, very old. Joe started to remember Hunter Island. At first he visualized tiny bits and pieces. Once he would suddenly realize he saw the old spring. Another time it would be the small island whose name Two Trees carried. The scenes came frequently and Joe did nothing to avoid them. Soon he was even dreaming of the old home. He welcomed the thoughts, and worked to enhance their vividness. It became an amusing game. He would think of one scene from his past life, just to see what other pictures it evoked from the deep well of memory.

Once, that game led him on a childhood walk with Eagle Feather. They passed through the grove of pines at the island's top, and started down toward the spring. Eagle Feather stopped and pointed at a dead, lightning-struck oak tree. Honey bees flew busily in and out through a large hole in one side of the hollow tree. The honey-filled combs could be seen from where he was standing. This was too much to pass up! The father sent his small son home to get a clay pot from the wigwam. The thought of sweet honeycomb to chew speeded the little boy along. When he returned with the pot, Eagle Feather had set several smoldering cattails near the hole. He explained that the smoke would have a calming effect on the bees. It would put them to sleep so the honey could be safely removed. He cautioned the boy that they should not take all the honey. Enough must be left for the bees or they would starve and die when winter came. The boy was already tasting the dark, amber sweetness on his tongue. They went to the hole and started, but before they had half filled their pot, the bees woke up. A cloud of angry insects followed them down the hill, through the marsh, and hovered over their submerged heads at the bay. The indignant bees finally left, but it was several hours before the two managed to retrieve the honey in the pot. They had a few bumps to remember the adventure, but as they ate honey that night, it didn't seem to matter. The hunters told their story to Small Doe and all three laughed happily about it.

One morning, Joe Two Trees packed his things and got into the dugout with Kane. He looked back toward the tall rock and watched it fall behind. The river was carrying him toward New York. He was on his way to visit Tony, but he was now fully aware that he would also go to the old home. It would be good to walk the remembered trails, and drink from his old spring. He wanted to stand, once more, inside the secret enclosure where he had been born. He would sit, once again, at the twin graves of Eagle Feather and Small Doe. It would please him to speak with his heart to them. He would tell of his great journey and that he was still Indian, in heart and deed. That last would be sure to please his spirit father who, even now, hunted in a happier place. Yes, he would visit Hunter Island. After that, he would know what to do.

The early part of his trip was uneventful, even relaxing, but in a short time, signs of man started to appear. The first evidence was patches of cleared land on the escarpment above him. They showed that farms hid farther back among the trees. By the end of his second day, people could be seen along the shore, and houses were all too frequent. Much woodland still stood between them, though, so Joe ignored the structures and concentrated his thoughts on the trees. By the fourth evening, he had some difficulty finding a deserted spot to make camp. He knew, then, that the next day would not end before he had reached the city. This thought came with mixed emotions. He had already noticed the queer looks he got from whites along the bank. He reasoned that the men had some right to be surprised at an Indian paddling by. He had felt all this once when he was only a boy. Surely he could run this same gauntlet again as a man.

Joe slept uneasily that last night on the river. He had found a spot where muddy swampland cut him off from the main bank. It was fairly secure, but he knew that men were all around, and not far off either. He pulled the small boat up on a mud flat and into tall reeds. Behind that dubious screen, he and Kane spent the dark hours in the boat.

When daylight allowed it, they traveled on. Before noon, the tall buildings on his left allowed no further doubt. He had entered the outskirts of the city. In a backwater swirl created by some small, rocky point that reached out into the river, Joe found what he wanted. It was a bulrush-choked cove that was hidden from above by a tall, sheer drop-off. Joe drove the canoe aground here and unloaded his things. Some of these he hid in a hasty cache, the rest, what little he would need for the walk to Tony's store, he laid aside for later. Then he ate, and fed the dog. It was easier to carry food in the stomach than on the back.

Now there remained but one more problem. If anyone came upon the boat, he would steal it and find the rest of his things. The boat was too obvious. It must be hidden well. Also, he wanted to be sure it would be here in the event he should have to make a quick escape. That had already happened, in this place, once.

Joe pondered for a time about the mushoon. If he hid it in the reeds, someone might still come across it. The place looked ideal for hunting ducks. It was not hard to visualize some hunter finding the boat and noticing it would be ideal for his particular use. Even if that didn't happen, a high, moon tide from the nearby sea could float the craft up and out of the reeds to be lost forever. No, it would not do to leave the boat simply concealed. It must somehow disappear; but how?

Then he remembered something that he had not thought about for a very long time. When Two Trees had been small, still only a baby really, Eagle Feather had once had this very problem. They had left Hunter Island then and paddled away in a canoe. When they reached the other shore, his father had hidden that boat so well that no one could have ever hoped to find it, except Eagle Feather himself. Two Trees smiled and walked to the boat with a purpose. He pushed it back into the water and started to fill it with round stones from the shoreline. It sank deeper and deeper until it was just barely afloat. Then he waded out, pushing the boat carefully in front of him. When he was standing chest deep in the river, he rocked the mushoon to and fro until water poured over the sides. When it did, displacing the air between the heavy rocks, the boat settled gently to the soft mud bottom. Joe smiled; he was sure it was safe now and he could refloat it in minutes if the need should arise.

18

The Attack

It was still early in the afternoon. Joe Two Trees called to Kane and the two set out along the banks. Joe felt safer near the river. Here, the city was not so close upon them. Woods and grassy meadows still existed. True, he passed people very frequently now, but he had begun to be used to the stares again. He just kept going along the city's fringe in spite of them. The dog, however, was another matter. She didn't like people at best, with the exception of her master. Each time a man or woman came into sight, she growled or snarled, begging to be ordered after them. Joe was quick to see the potential danger in this. Eventually, she was almost sure to misinterpret some harmless move by one of the whites as a threat against Joe. She would then be duty-bound to attack and kill.

Joe had had enough of killing in this city. He wanted to avoid trouble at any cost. He sat down and, using his knife, cut long strips of deerskin from the excess material along the seams of his trousers. He tied these into a looped leash for Kane. She had never felt the cut of rope around her neck and first she shied away from the loop. But when she understood that it was a thing her master wanted of her, she accepted.

The shoreline was changing here. Roads led to it and ended at wooden piers. In some spots, boats were tied up. One dock looked more familiar than the rest. Joe gazed back along the road that led up to it, and he was reasonably sure it was the one he had run down on a long-ago night. The area had changed.

He noticed that there now seemed to be fewer buildings of wood. Those that remained had a ramshackle look. New, taller buildings of brick and stone had begun to predominate. One thing was still the same, though. Everyone rushed from place to place, appearing very concerned over something. They hardly even seemed to notice him. This pleased Two Trees. Here and there, though, someone would stare at the dog. Joe smiled inwardly at the looks of fear she evoked. It was good that they realized she was a force to be considered. When last he walked these same streets, he had no such protection.

It was only a few blocks now. Joe wondered what Tony's reaction would be. He hoped the shopkeeper wouldn't be angry or disappointed that Two Trees hadn't sought out his uncle in Staten Island. But as he thought about it, Joe was sure the man wouldn't mind. He had sent Joe there to save him, and fate had accomplished that end. So Tony's purpose had been realized. No, Tony would be glad to see Joe. They would sit and tell each other stories of the many years. Tony would have coffee for them to drink.

As he visualized the happy reunion, Joe became fully convinced that he had done the right thing in coming here. Then he remembered the silver coins he had left with Tony. He could use these to buy supplies for the coming winter. A new pair of boots, especially, would be welcome. He wouldn't ask Tony for the money though. If he had forgotten it or chose to keep it as Joe once offered, Two Trees would understand. He owed the man for his help to a young Indian boy.

He turned a corner, and across the street was the old alley that had once been his home. It was too much to disregard. Joe found that he couldn't pass without taking the time to stop and reminisce. By the force of old habit, he looked to make sure no one was watching and then walked into the gloomy shadows. As he reached the end, Joe marveled. It seemed as though no one had walked here since the day he had left. The trees still stood, blocking the spot from the rear. Leaves were still blown by some quirk of the wind into the very corner where he once slept away cold winter nights. He noticed the spot where his enemy's body had fallen. The rains of many seasons had long since washed away the bloodstains. The Indian thought grimly about that and decided it had probably taken the rain a long time to finish this particular work. He reached into his shirt and drew out the flint knife. Its blade still glittered in the faltering light with some strange life all its own. Joe turned and tucked the knife away. It was growing dark, and he wanted to get to Tony's before the store was closed for the night.

As he started back out of the alley, something stopped him. He turned and looked again. Someone *had* been here since that day! When he had left, Joe had been in a hurry. He had scooped his silver out of the hole near the trees and left its rock cover lying to one side. He had not taken the time to reseal the hole, because that would serve no purpose except to delay him. Now the stone sat neatly, flush with the ground around it. Someone had closed the hole, and quite carefully at that.

He walked back to the rock and stood in the shadows of the old trees. Joe stooped and pulled at the rock. He was correct in thinking the cover had been well reset. He gave it one strong tug and it popped loose. There, amid the water-ravaged remains of a paper bag, Joe saw the distinctive sheen of silver. He reached in and extracted the dollars. It looked to be about the same number that Tony had promised to save for him. This was amazing! What strange thing had happened here during the years of his travels? The only people who had ever known about this hiding hole were Tony and the two surviving thieves. Tony had once asked if Joe kept his pay money in a safe place, and Joe had told him about his little spot. The thieves, of course, had seen it for themselves. It was certain that they would not come here to put money into Joe's cache. This must mean that the money had been buried by Tony. But this made no sense. Why would he do so when the silver would certainly be safer in his own store, a few blocks away?

This was all too confusing. Joe trotted away toward the store, the coins making a heavy jingling noise as he went. He rounded the last corner and stopped abruptly. Tony's store looked different. It was larger and its front had changed. Then Joe saw why. It had grown to include the small shop that had formerly stood next to it, attached but separated by a wall. Now, the two were one single large store. Something was wrong here. Two Trees sensed immediately that something different than Tony's store was behind those shiny, new windows. Then the door opened, and two men staggered to the street unsteadily. Through the briefly opened door, Joe heard music and laughter. It was a barroom. Had quiet Tony, the shopkeeper, opened a bar? It didn't make sense.

Joe crossed the street to the door, but hesitated out front. He wanted to go inside and ask for his old friend, but he was afraid. The noise, the idea of being enclosed with all those white men, these weighed heavily upon him. There was Kane, though. They would keep their distance from her. Then too, how else could he hope to find Tony? The dog tried to pull him away, past this place of bad scents. There was sweat, whiskey, dirt, men, beer, and a host of smells that made her broad muscled shoulders bristle. She must have been upset that he held her here. She wanted him to leave with her and whined her plea, but Joe hushed her. He mustered up all the confidence he owned and pushed through the door.

Joe walked inside and stopped to look around the room. As he did, so did everything else stop. The piano ceased its tinkle. Glasses were held poised in front of mouths. Conversations halted in midword. While this silence endured, every eye in the house watched the woodsman and his dog. Joe knew he presented an unusual sight for these city dwellers, but he hadn't expected this reaction. His hair had grown long during the summer on the river. It hung dark and straight to his shoulders. His clothing consisted of buckskin and fur. His feet were covered by hand-crafted moccasins. The belt around his middle was made from the skin of a very large snake. Also, there was the growling, black giant at his side. Joe reconsidered. Perhaps the reaction of these city men was not so strange after all. He forced his weathered features into a smile. This seemed to be the signal for all to return to their previous activities. The music and drinking resumed, and Joe relaxed a bit. He was aware of the frequent glances that still came his way, however.

Joe went to an open place along the bar and waited for the bartender to come to him. He planned only to ask for the whereabouts of Tony. The bartender cut him short by telling him he would have to tie the dog outside. Joe tried to protest this, but the man seemed quite adamant. He would neither serve nor speak to Joe until this was done. Recognizing it as unavoidable, the Indian complied. Kane protested as Joe tied her lead to one of the iron rings on the stone hitching posts, but he calmed her down. She agreed to stay, but her yellow eyes told him it was done against her better judgment. Joe went in again, and the man's smile told him he had been wise to do as he was told. The sound of silver in Joe's pouch may also have been responsible for the smile.

The man asked what Joe would have to drink. Joe responded that he didn't like whiskey. The bartender walked off and returned a few seconds later with a frothy mug of beer. Joe hadn't actually ordered it, but he realized that refusal would not be a good way to start out if he hoped to obtain any information. He reached into his pouch and gave a dollar. Soon, it was replaced by a pile of smaller coins. Joe remembered the time Tony had explained the idea of "change." Perhaps this man was an honest one, too. Did his eyes linger a bit too long on Joe's pouch though?

Joe was intrigued by the golden liquid. He watched the way bubbles rose from no particular source in the glass and joined the white foam at top. He noticed many similar drinks along the bar. If all these men drank it, it couldn't be something to fear. He decided to try it. He raised the mug to his lips and sipped. It was nothing like the fiery liquid that had once caused him to cough and be ridiculed. This was different, cool, almost pleasant. He took another, larger gulp. It was pleasing to the tongue. It grew tastier with each further draught. Somehow, several more mugs found their way to Joe's hand before he remembered his original purpose. He had started to feel a very pleasant warmth. He would ask about Tony, as soon as the bartender stopped running back and forth bringing beer. He knew he would get around to it, but the beer tasted so good. What difference would one more make? The time came when Joe knew that if he didn't ask now, he would forget. He called out loudly, and the man came over. Joe was finding it odd that he had trouble saying words. This hadn't happened to him in a very long time. He spoke English as well as he spoke Algonquin. Then, he suddenly remembered the naming of Kane. He didn't speak Algonquin any longer. The thought had a sobering effect.

"Where is Tony?" asked the Indian. The question was answered by the blank smile every bartender reserves for meaningless prattle from inebriated patrons. Joe asked again, and slowly, ever so slowly, he made the man understand that he actually wanted some reply beyond the inane smile. The man told Joe he had never heard of any person called Tony who had his shop here. When he came from Ireland, relatives had taken him to see the two vacant buildings. With some help from them, he bought and made one large place from the former two. He gestured around with his arms and said, "As you can well see, my wild friend." Joe felt some slight insult in the words, but the man's smile and the beer's effect put that out of mind.

Even drunk, his brain deduced what was probably the simple truth of the situation. Tony had tired of shopkeeping, for one of many possible reasons. He had left for another place then. It could have been the uncle's farm or Italy or any other place. Joe knew then that he would never see the Italian again. The man was gone, lost to him forever, somewhere along the many years and miles of life. But when he was ready to leave, Tony had thought of Joe. If the boy ever did come back, he would need money. Tony had probably taken the silver, very secretly, to the alley and left it. Joe smiled. Tony had been a fiercely honest man, that he already knew. The silver offered further proof. Joe silently hoped that Tony had found a better place for himself. It would not be hard, thought the Indian part of him, to find a better place than this city. He thanked the bartender politely and turned toward the door.

Even before he reached the street, Joe knew something was wrong. He could hear Kane crying wildly. When he pushed out to the street, the sight unnerved even Joe. Her ears were flat against her skull. The hair along her entire back bristled straight and stiff as a porcupine's, and she stood upright almost strangled by the leash.

Joe ran toward Kane to release the rope, but he never reached the hysterical animal. Something hard hit him on the side of his head. He wasn't unconscious, but he couldn't keep to his feet. As Two Trees fell, he recognized the sticky warmth of blood running down his scalp and neck. He hit the hard cobblestone street and tried to rise. He couldn't. Another blow from the same heavy instrument fell.

Time passed. Seconds, minutes, hours may have passed. Gradually, by slow degrees, Joe became aware that he was still alive. His first impression was one of wetness and a roaring noise in his ears. He thought he was lying facedown in the river, drowning. Then he pulled his head up and realized that the wet was his own blood. A large puddle had accumulated under his face and made mud with the dirt of the street. Joe had almost died, drowned in it. Then he turned his face to locate the source of the unfamiliar roar. A large circle of men stood around him. They yelled and screamed, but mixed with their sounds was the howl of Kane. She stood over the helpless Indian, ready to kill or die before anyone would be able to touch her fallen master, and none was so foolish as to try. Joe struggled to get up and realized he was badly hurt. He wasn't yet sure if any bones were broken, but several teeth were splintered, and many deep cuts covered his body. He could feel that innumerable boots had left their mark on his sides, back, and head. He fell back to the street and was sick. The muscular spasms of vomiting left him weaker, and in more pain than before. Slowly, the crowd evaporated into the night. First by ones, then by twos and threes, he was left alone. The fun was over. The spectacle was finished. They went home to their pipes and porridge, wives and wine. There was nothing to watch except the last few drops of blood draining from the body of an obscure stranger. It was late.

The dog stayed by the bleeding man, ready to die of hunger by his side if he didn't rise before that happened. Through the night she stood her watch, knowing no other thought than the man. She licked his face clean and nuzzled him with her cool, wet nose. By dawn, even Kane was sure he would die. She started to cry, as only an animal can. She grieved, deep in her body, for the lost master. Her cries traveled a long, soft route through her flesh, and by the time they reached her throat, they were only tiny sounds. Those were the sounds Joe Two Trees finally heard as he woke.

Joe rolled over feebly. His hand went to a long gash along his throat. Blood was still pumping from the deep cut, but he didn't notice that. His hand found the thong around his neck and followed it from end to end. The tooth of Konoh was gone! He rose to his knees and searched, hand over hand, from one cobble to the next. It was gone. They had taken his totem thing. He also noticed that the pouch of silver was missing. That seemed not so important. The tooth of the cave bear was his manhood, strength. They had taken it. Joe fell back to the street, unconscious. When he woke again, it was already full light. They had not done the thing they set out to do. He would not let them do it now. His fingers found the haft of his knife. They had missed it! Holding its reassuring handle, he drifted between life and death.

Joe came more alert with the coming day. He pulled himself to his knees, using the dog for balance. She tried to help in every way possible, but it amounted only to whimpering and supporting his weight. In time he was able to rise to a shaky, standing position. Crouching, with a hand still resting on the dog's shoulder, he took a few steps. It surprised him to find that he was able to do this. Each breath drawn into his lungs was painful. No doubt he had sustained several broken ribs. One leg hurt badly. It was probably broken also, but by resting his weight on the dog, he could still use it somewhat to support him. His left hand was useless. Some boot had crushed its bones during the attack. Most of the cuts had crusted closed. Only the really deep ones still oozed blood.

Two Trees took mental stock of his condition, and some inner yardstick of survival told him he had not reached the mark that spelled out death. Joe was satisfied. Neither happy nor sad, simply satisfied. For one who had survived till now on the strength of wits alone, survival was not a happening to be celebrated. It should be accepted. That is how Joe reacted to it.

Kane supported him as he limped to the river. There, he splashed water in his face. He didn't wash out his many wounds. That would only open them and cause more loss of blood, a thing he couldn't spare right now. The river gave him hope. Joe remembered the hidden place and the canoe. That was where he would try to go. Man and dog turned upstream to retrace their earlier steps. If they had gotten strange glances a day earlier, the looks were now openly hostile. He ignored them. Once, several young boys threw stones at Joe and Kane. He couldn't contain the deep anger any longer. Joe loosened the leash and sent the dog after them. In a few minutes, she returned with rich, red color around her mouth. He felt not the smallest twinge of guilt or sorrow. He was almost ashamed of what he felt.

Joe was about to put the leash back on Kane's neck, but something kept him from it. She was a fierce, brave one, a lover of freedom. The leash was wrong. He prepared to throw it in the flowing river but stopped. Something about its end caught his eye. It had been cut! He stopped and examined it carefully. There was no doubt. It was cut off clean, as only a knife could do. Until now, he had naturally assumed that Kane had chewed it through. He looked at the end for a third time. It was cut. That meant that someone in the crowd had turned Kane loose. Why?

Joe wondered about it as they made their way upriver. Someone had released his dog, so that she could save him. It would have taken very few more kicks to kill. He knew no one there. Why would a white do such a thing for an Indian? He owed his life to some anonymous white back there. Joe was to wonder over these puzzles for a great number of years and never find an answer. Armed with that knowledge, Joe tried to keep from hating every American he saw. It didn't work. The information passed through his mind and faded from importance. It had happened. He was alive. There was no further value to it. To stay alive was now the imperative that governed his body and mind. That would, at best, not be easy.

He tripped and stumbled many times, blinded by blood that found courses from the many scalp wounds, into his eyes. Often, the dog licked him back to consciousness. If not for her, he would have stopped, to bleed to death along the way, or be arrested and bleed to death in jail. The movement of walking was deeply painful, but the hurt that occurred when he fell was much worse. It was the goad that kept Two Trees on his feet.

Gradually, he made progress to the north. As the houses grew farther apart, Joe started to feel a strength of wild places pervade his injured body. He walked through the night, afraid to stop. He knew that rest would only serve to stiffen him, like the wounded deer. If he lay down to sleep he knew he would be unable to rise with the light of day. He must be in a safe place before he catered to the wounds that covered him. If he did not reach the protected beach where the canoe was hidden before resting, he would not reach it at all.

This was not the place or way that fate, or his Tchi-Manitou, had chosen for the death of the last Bronx Algonquin, however.

The primal strength of his Indian spirit forced Two Trees on, and past the known limits of his endurance, on again. At some point along his way, the pain itself, as extreme injuries sometimes do, became its own anesthetic. By the very intensity of its strength, it numbed itself and allowed him to go forward. The man and dog inched along, periodically wading into the river to draw strength from its chilly water. Joe knew that the spirits of Manetto, the evil entity, walked at night. It was important to keep going. When light came, most of these spirits would go back to their cave and be replaced by those of light. Joe preferred that his fate should ultimately be in the hands of those more friendly spirits.

A cold wind brought drizzle with the dawn. Joe hardly noticed. He was thinking about the future. Even as they walked uptown along the river, Joe Two Trees decided that there would in fact be a future. His body yearned for rest, but something else drove him on. He needed a goal in order to keep going, and his mind was starting to provide it.

The day was no longer young when Kane and Joe stumbled to the security of the hidden cove. Joe struggled down the steep embankment, more falling than not, and arrived at the place where he had left his things only a day ago. He scrambled into the hidden place and gathered forth the skin of his great bear. Wrapping himself in this medicine thing, he slept within seconds. Kane placed her body against him and gave what little she had, her warmth. Joe knew nothing of it; only time would now tell if he would ever wake again.

Day came, dull and wet. Joe did not stir. The dog seemed nervous, but she stood and waited. Instinct told her sleep would do more to heal her master than anything she could do. Later in the morning he woke. The muscles had stiffened, broken bones swollen, but life was still there. When Kane saw that he was awake, she licked his face until he sat. Joe tried to move various parts of his body. He counted many bones that he knew were broken. Then he felt with his good hand at the deep cuts over his body. He became aware that many of these were knife cuts. Several still oozed blood, more than one full day later. He objectively judged his chances of survival. They were poor.

Here, in front of a crackling fire, it was easy for me, a young boy, to ask questions about survival. I asked if he wasn't afraid. Joe answered simply, "Yes." As ancient as he was, a straightness had come to his back and shoulders. The talk of fighting for life had awakened things in the old man. He tried to explain them. He had done his best. He had worked toward life. After this, there was only one thing left, the will of his God. When Joe managed to reach the cove and find his bearskin, he had done all that the Maker could ask. Now came that Spirit's turn. Joe pointed out that each man must eventually come to a point, where having done his utmost, he awaits the verdict of the Almighty. That was the point Joe had reached. The outcome of his sleep depended on something, but it wasn't his strength, the weather, or any other fact humans count as important. The issue had entered other realms.

19

Monatun

Somehow, I have never forgotten the few moments that separated the part of the story he had just told from what was yet to come. It sits in my mind still, like an intermission, separating two parts of a play. Until now, he had been telling me the history of a young man, unbeaten, indomitable. Now, the story seemed to fall with the death of the fire before us. As I watched the flames burn down, I was sure of two things. One was that I would never hear anything more important. The other was that I would be in deep trouble when I went home this night. I knew it, but I chose to disregard the fact.

The idea of a worried mother and father paled before the scene that was opening for me here. I watched the sick man as he strained for the strength to continue. Great things were happening here, and by some granted power, I was given the privilege to be fascinated by them.

The man was hard put about how to continue. He wanted to explain that he hated all white men. That was difficult if you consider that I was his sole audience. He managed.

The man and dog stayed in the spot Joe had originally chosen. His instincts had been good. When he took the boat ashore, Joe had looked the area over with an unconscious eye to survival. Now that foresight was his salvation. The overhanging cliff kept him hidden from people above. The thick reeds screened him from the boat traffic on the river. Several times, he could hear strollers on the walk above him, but they went past. Every time this happened, he smiled. He had beaten them, and he grew stronger. It was fortunate that the supply of dried deer meat was sufficient, because during the first weeks, hunting would have been impossible for him. Slow progress made him able to rise for walks that got a bit longer each day. The torn flesh and splintered bones of the young Indian were healing. In several more weeks he would be able to travel on. He knew his destination now, or perhaps his destiny. It was Hunter Island. Joe wished he had thought to bring the medicine with him when he left that home. He remembered Eagle Feather's advice, "Use this only when there is no other way, my son, for when it is finished, there can never be more again." Perhaps it was best that he had not taken the medicine. He would certainly have used it. Now, it still remained, safe and intact, in its stone stronghold at the old home.

A disturbing reality became more obvious to Joe day by day. The hours of light were growing shorter with each cycle of the sun. Soon Indian summer would end. The days of warmth and comfort were almost over for this year. Even though his body was not fully prepared yet, he would have to move on soon. When he reached Hunter Island, there would be much to do. Joe saw clearly that the ancient story had been very true. The Great Spirit was offering Indian summer, the time when he stopped the progress of seasons, so that Joe could prepare for winter. It was as if his father was reminding him of the day when he had taken Two Trees to the wooded hill. There, Eagle Feather had shown the boy the many signs of autumn. When dusk was falling, Eagle Feather pointed to sun spirit and showed the boy how far south he had traveled to set. He told Two Trees that even though that spirit tried mightily, as evidenced by his bright red color, only feeble warmth came back to them. When sun spirit began his crooked walk, lower and lower to the horizon each day, a wise Indian prepared for what would soon come. But although he felt pleasure in these old thoughts of boyhood, he also found a command. Move now, otherwise you will face starvation and death.

During that night, Joe weighed his options. They were few, but life had taught him that it often depended upon some very insignificant detail. He was reasonably sure that he could find

his way back to Hunter Island by foot. Once, long ago, he had
gotten to this city that way. But there were drawbacks. The
miles would not be easy on his partially healed bones. Then,
too, there would be the white men along his way. Joe knew that
if they interfered with him, he would use both dog and knife.
He wanted no more blood or killing.

On the other hand, there was the boat. He had never seen the
water route around this island and back to his home, but he
had the old stories to guide him. Joe knew that he must go to
the end of this Manhattan Island, then north and east. The
fishermen from Snak-a-pins had traveled to a place called
Monatun, where whirlpools and currents were powerful. That
should be easy to find. He would use it as a landmark. Once he
had passed through Monatun, he would be nearly in sight of
Snak-a-pins. His father had taken him there as a boy. He would
know it when he saw it again. It was late when he slept, but he
did so in a peace born of knowledge. He would wade into the
river tomorrow and float the canoe.

Day broke gray with cold rain, but Joe was glad about it.
The mist and sheets of driven spray would make him less visible as he passed the shores of the city. He waded into the water,
surprised by its coldness. Winter was closer than he had hoped.
But he managed to use his good leg to push enough rocks out of
the mushoon so that by standing on one side, he could roll it
over and let it float to the top. Then he righted the little boat
and pulled it to shore. Soon, he had it emptied and ready for its
journey.

He loaded his scant equipment and he and the dog stepped
aboard. It was easy to push off into the river, and the current
soon had them. All that was needed was the occasional paddle
thrust to keep away from the banks. It was well that the river
did most of the work here, because Joe soon knew that his
injured hand was not healed enough. Going downstream would
present little problem, but when he rounded the island, Joe
knew he might be required to go against the flow, upstream.
What then? An idea started to form, and he decided to imple-
ment it now rather than wait until it was crucial. He had the
leash that he had made for Kane. With it he lashed the paddle
along his left forearm. That would allow him to use the
strength of his arm without using the broken hand. Would it

work? Joe dipped the paddle and forced it through the water. It
was clumsy, even a little painful, but the bow responded. It
would do. Wet and cold though he was in the early winter
northeaster, Joe smiled happily. The river would not wash him
into the ocean to die. He had won once more at this game of
survival. These men had not yet killed Two Trees. Through
him the Indian race still lived! The smile broadened to a laugh
muffled and lost amid the rain and wind. Kane looked up happily and waved her tail at the sound of the master's laughter.

The storm worsened through the day, but the graceful little
boat was at home on the current of the Hudson. Its low profile
caught little wind, and its upturned bow cut most of the waves
cleanly. When he realized how well the canoe performed, Joe
was glad he had spent the extra days for detail work on this
craft. As he reached the end of the island, Joe saw that the
waves were still rising. The possibility of swamping was immi-
nent and would be a poor way to spend the dusk hours. He
decided that safety should now take precedence over haste. He
would land now and spend this night ashore.

But where? There was no spot on the island-city where he
would spend this or any other night. Danger existed on the
storm-ripped river, but he would risk it before the city. He
looked away from shore, and through a rent in the thick
squalls, he caught sight of something. Then the storm closed
again and he lost it. Had it been an island? Joe turned the boat
away from the sheltering shore to seek it out. Through some
combination of skill and luck, he found the island in the mists.

Joe pulled the boat ashore, above the raging wave line, and
found a sheltered spot among the rocks. There, covered by his
bearskin, man and dog weathered the blow. After a while, the
wind began to shift. It now came from northwest instead of
northeast. It was amazing that those few degrees of direction
could have such dramatic effect on the weather. The temperature fell rapidly. A brilliant clearing arc formed below the western clouds and pushed them away. As the last ragged clouds
passed overhead, their final raindrops fell as snow. Joe walked
around the barren little island. He could do that in a very short
time. It was nothing much to speak of really, only a pile of
rocks. He smiled. It would serve for the night.

The dry north wind brought a bracing chill. He managed to

start a small fire with the damp driftwood along the shore. It dried his clothing quickly. Dried out and warm, Joe walked his little island. When he looked toward the city, Two Trees had the impulse to shake his fist at it, but he resisted. He was free now. He would leave the city and its people behind him. Indian Joe was reborn that morning as Two Trees, Algonquin. That was to be the way he saw himself until he finally joined his ancestors.

The next day dawned cold. The stiff breeze ruffled New York harbor and gave its water a look of nervous motion. Joe noticed clouds of sea birds hovering, diving in various places along the shores. Then the morning sun caught flashing color under one of the nearer clouds. The group of birds pushed toward Joe. They were frantic, in pursuit of something. As they came closer, he saw that the birds were screeching and diving over a huge school of fish. The fish cornered their prey against one side of Joe's island and thousands of mullet ran aground among the weed-covered rocks. Joe watched large fish chase after them, and be beached as the waves receded. The predators were striped bass. Thousands of pounds of food lay squirming among the rocks. Joe availed himself of the chance. He gilled a large fish and dragged it to the dry land. It would make a fine meal for him and Kane.

Joe walked back to the tide line and marveled at the many schools of bass that were visible from where he stood. He had often fished for the bass with Eagle Feather, but hadn't imagined that so many of them could possibly exist. Now that he saw the massed, migratory schools, he felt strong respect for their tribe. Each year they left Hunter Island in the fall and reappeared in the spring. Two Trees had often wondered where they went. Now he saw that they met here, in groups, to form themselves into one great clan. Later he watched the schools go up the river. He had come from there, and he wondered where such great numbers of fish would find room to swim abreast in even this broad waterway.

He watched more schools of bass enter the harbor. Some came down the river that he would soon travel to reach Monatun, the Place of Dangerous Waters. Others came from the ocean beyond. Again, the surrounding shores were dotted with umbrella-shaped canopies of sea birds. It was amazing to watch the vast groups of fish enter the bay, gather and proceed upriver. Joe was impressed by their apparent purposefulness. The mass seemed to be governed by some intelligence far greater than that of any single fish. They acted in unison to herd and trap the small food fish, then, when all had eaten well, the bass joined together for their journey north. In the distance, he could see numbers of small boats. The frequent silver flash of sunlight off broad bass scales indicated that men were catching fish from the boats. Joe wasn't surprised. Such great numbers of fish would be obvious even to the city men.

A large school was feeding right in front of Joe and he watched as clouds of bait fish erupted into the waiting birds above. Suddenly, faster than his eye could follow, a path was sliced through the gulls by a hurtling body from higher up. It never slacked its speed, but grazed the water with long talons and reversed direction. It climbed slower than it had dived—the large eagle now carried a striped bass nearly as heavy as the one Joe had captured earlier. She carried her prize to a tall rock nearby and quickly started to devour it. The curved claws and powerful, hooked beak made short work of the fish. Soon she had eaten the choicest parts and would leave the rest for later. The chance provided by the annual, fall migration was too great to lose by spending her time on a single fish.

She rose on broad wings until Joe could only discern her as a speck against the cloudless, delft-colored sky. This time Joe watched closely, hoping to see her majestic dive in its entirety. She circled slowly, surveying the pandemonium of schools below. She chose one. Her mighty wings folded and the sky hunter became a projectile. Her speed increased as she fell, and again she rose with a large bass securely skewered between her claws. Joe smiled at her success. The feathered creature was a powerful totem animal to the Indians who once lived here. He was happy for her. She would feed and be strong, to raise her fledglings in the spring. This was good, for during the years, reflected the man, he had noticed fewer and fewer eagles. This creature that had once given its name to Two Trees's father seemed to have left the places where white men came to live.

Joe cooked his fish over the coals of the fire. Later, he and Kane filled their stomachs. He was glad for the opportunity of a good meal. It would give strength for the journey still ahead.

Joe noticed that the tide was now in his favor. It would help him along toward Monatun. So the two set off up the East River, passing school after school of striped bass. Joe crossed to the easterly side, where there were fewer signs of men. There were houses, but green patches still stood, in contrast to the gray walls of Manhattan. Joe Two Trees paddled along, under an open, unobstructed sky. No bridge had yet been built to join these shores.

On he went, northward, hugging the shore now, to avoid the growing current. The river was becoming so swift here that Joe felt certain he must be nearing Monatun (which the white man calls Hell Gate). The old stories spoke of this place as being dangerous in the extreme. It held moving whirlpools so strong that they might easily swallow up a canoe. The current ran in two directions at the same time. The result of this was a violent, confused area of huge waves that might break unpredictably at any time or place within the passageway. All in all, if the old tales proved true, Joe knew he was in for a difficult stretch, but he reserved any opinion until he could see with his own eyes what confronted him. He forced on against the swift, seething flow. Here, he could not even avoid it by staying near the banks. The current's force extended right to the edges, and protruding rocks near shore made it perilous. He was forced to stay closer to the middle now. He rounded a projection of land, and ahead he saw Monatun. There was no possible mistake, and it was every bit as fearsome as it must have been in the days of his ancestors. Their stories had exaggerated little, if at all. Joe had reached Hell Gate, the graveyard of many a vessel much larger than his.

His first impression on seeing it was one of utter impenetrability. He steered the canoe into the back eddy of a huge boulder. There, he wedged his bow into a cleft in the stone. The current held him in place as well as any anchor. He wanted time to examine this evil-looking water and decide his course of action.

Joe saw the reason for the great currents at first glance. The two sides of the river were constricted here, like the neck of a bottle. At each turn of tide, the vast waters of Long Island Sound were forced to funnel into the river and then the sea. That great volume of water was simply too much to fit comfortably between the narrowed, rocky shores. The result was that the Sound piled higher than the river below it, causing tortured flumes and mighty pressures as it forced through. These would not be relieved until the Sound waters reached a condition of equilibrium with the river. At that point, the turning tide would reverse the situation, piling seawater into the river to accumulate at Hell Gate and force its way back into the Sound.

To make matters worse, tides in the different bodies of water were influenced by either Sound or ocean tides. Since these are never synchronous, the incoming river tide met the still outgoing Sound tide head on, right here at Monatun. The result of all this was a maelstrom of fury.

The Indian was not happy with the facts his observations had served to gather. This spot had every sign of being impassable. The actual length of the constriction was short; Joe could see that if the water was calm, he would be able to traverse it in a few minutes. It wasn't calm, though, and it might just as well have been a thousand miles long.

To abandon his water route toward the old home now could prove to be disastrous. The side of the river where he was now would bring him onto the long sandy land across the water from Hunter Island. From there, it would be extremely difficult ever to recross the Sound without his canoe. If he crossed to the Manhattan side and struck out on foot, he would be in danger from several sources. First, and perhaps most feared, was the menace of now-hated whites. Then, there was the fact that his poorly healed bones might very well be incapable of sustaining his weight for a long overland trek. It was not without some regrets that Joe saw the inevitable. He would either pass through Monatun, or his eventual fate would be a different one than he had planned.

Joe leaned his weight back against the bundled skin of Konoh the bear. The feeling of it against his shoulders was good. Perhaps some strange magic flowed into the man from its presence, for at that moment he realized that no schools of bass were in view. This seemed somewhat curious in its suddenness. It made him look around for a reason. He hadn't thought the movement of the fish to be important to his problem, so Joe had failed to notice the exact time when they stopped coming downriver. Now, he thought more about that fact. They obviously swam with the tide! No fish, given a choice, would swim against this racing force. Then he looked at the rock that held his canoe. A wide expanse of seaweed-covered stones was visible above the water line. It was nearly low water! The thought came as a great revelation. He had unconsciously assumed that in this place of unnatural waters, other laws of nature were also suspended. They were not. The unfailing tides still rose and fell, governed by some timepiece greater than any that man had ever made. Low tide was almost here. It was then that Joe must make his try, for any other time would mean sure disaster. The really bad factor was the tide overrun, when the incoming waters met the outgoing. Here, at Monatun, there was no period of truly slack tide. Should he be unlucky enough to be at the wrong place when the two actual tides met, the only outcome possible would be catastrophe. But no other choice was given. He prepared himself in the old Indian ways.

Joe had never watched a complete cycle of tides in this place, and he had no real knowledge of the right time. The hour, minute, and second that he chose were arbitrary, but the moment came when he deemed circumstances to be most favorable. He freed the boat and pointed it into the still-seething waters. He made good progress at first, and could almost see the end of this peril ahead. Then, a series of sharp waves appeared to his left, and even as he angled into them, he could tell it was too late. He cut through the first and biggest, but the bow dropped as it passed under his canoe. The next one curled over the upthrust wood and poured a large amount of water into the boat. The dog gave a small yelp at the feel of cold water. Joe forced the now-sluggish craft back to his original course and worked to make her cut forward. Now, however, she rode low in the water, no longer the sleek, light boat of a few seconds ago. Joe pushed at the paddle with desperate determination. He gained, but with great effort. Then he looked ahead and saw the gently swelling waters of the Sound. He was almost there! The sight gave him renewed strength, and the distance diminished steadily. Then, a long, low wave approached from ahead. There was no avoiding it. He could do no more than meet it and pray. The comber chose the precise instant of meeting his boat in which to crest. It rolled white

oamy water over the entire length of the mushoon. Joe was
swamped.

The dog paddled along next to him as Joe grabbed for the
floating boat. It floated, but only even with the water's surface.
The current had them now, and nothing he could do would
have any effect. Joe held the boat and floated at the mercy of
the tides. He spotted the paddle nearby and swam to grab it. He
was able to regain his hold on the boat, but only with difficulty.
No other item could lure him away after that experience. Then,
floating a good distance off, he saw the bearskin. He judged the
speed of the current and length of water, and saw that he would
not be able to drag it back even if he reached it. He followed it
with sad eyes as it drifted away and was lost. When it was gone
from sight, it seemed to take on a meaning more important
than during the years he had loved it. Now he thought of it as a
harbinger of his doom. Having won the prize, only to lose it,
was an almost certain sign from the Maker. Joe made mental
preparations for his death.

The cold water was weakening him rapidly, and in a short
time he was nearly unconscious. Now and then he would look
up and think he saw things in the waves ahead. First it was a
bear, rising to attack. Next he saw men with clubs and knives.
A shock of recognition pulled him awake! There, just ahead,
was Eagle Feather in the old canoe. Just as when Two Trees
was a small child, the father paddled ahead of him. He spoke
the old words of encouragement again. It was as it had been.
Eagle Feather used to paddle Two Trees out into the Sound and
drop him overboard. Then, keeping the canoe a scant distance
ahead, he would make the boy swim to shore. Two Trees remembered that he had cried, and said he was drowning, but he
had always been able to follow the father. The crying had
stopped after many such lessons, and he had not drowned. But
something else had come of Eagle Feather's training. This boy,
this Indian, was a fine swimmer. Two Trees remembered all
this as he watched the father pull away from him. He took the
filled canoe by its bow and powerfully followed Eagle Feather.

The time came when the father's words were distant and
indistinct. Joe could tell that he was not able to keep up any
longer. At last, he lost Eagle Feather in a swirl of fog. The
Indian was certain that his end had come. But the dog barked,

waking him from his stupor. She grabbed his sleeve and yanked at it insistently. The semiconscious man wished this annoyance would go away and leave him to his rest. She wouldn't. She pulled until she knew that it would not wake him. Then, she boldly took the flesh of her master between her teeth and bit. It had the effect which she hoped. He jerked awake and glared at her. In doing this, he saw that he had pushed his chest up from a bottom. He was on shore! He had been about to drown and die in six inches of water. Joe grabbed Kane and hugged her furiously, ignoring the blood running from the wound she had inflicted in order to save him.

Joe crawled the rest of the way to dry land and collapsed. While he slept, the dry wind and warm dog saved his life. When he woke, his clothes were still damp, and the air temperature was cold. This discomfort was a pleasant sensation for Two Trees; much better than the pervasive cold he had felt in the river. He stood to see what had actually happened and where he was.

What he saw did little to encourage him. He had been pushed well east in the Sound, and had accidentally come up on a small rocky knoll. The sun was nearly gone, and soon he would face a night on this tiny rock with no hope of food, fire, or warmth. He had only the dog, Kane, the paddle, and the flint knife, which had miraculously stayed inside his belt. That last item had remained, strangely in his grip, even as he washed ashore. He looked to the waters that surrounded him. Another small island lay a short distance away, and on its rock shore Joe could see the canoe, rising and falling as waves hit it.

There was salvation! The thought was both happy and grim. Was the boat still sound? She sat, bouncing on the rocks at the whim of every wave. If those rocks had pounded holes into her bottom, she would serve no further purpose to Two Trees. Also, the boat was several hundred feet away, across the cold water. Could he force himself back into the water? Could he muster the strength to swim across? Doubts swept his mind. They were put to rest soon enough by a gruesome fact. If he did not swim to the boat and find it intact, Joe would spend a short time on the island. Death by freezing or starvation would soon end his stay. The doubts were natural, but the choice was an easy one.

He wasted little time. Joe called Kane to his side and made a running dive. The momentum carried him into deep water, and there he started stroking toward the barren rock that held his boat. Cold crept into his already weakened body with the stealth of a hunting wolf. Once inside, it gnawed at his vital organs, causing cramps and other pain. Midway, he felt that reaching the shore was no longer possible. Joe sensed the presence of death. He was not surprised. This dark aura had hovered near him ever since the bearskin had been lost.

But another dark angel swam closer by. He was able to seize a fistful of her hair, and together they continued toward the rock. Joe fought for the strength to rise and walk upright to the dry ground. Somewhere in his heritage, surely not in his damaged body, he found it.

Shivering wildly, the man went straight to the small, hollow boat. Its shell was fragile. He had built it and knew its weaknesses well. As he approached, Joe tried to keep himself from hoping for a miracle. That way, disappointment might be easier to endure. He reached it. It was badly bruised in several places, and rocks had splintered sections of gunwale, but the all-important hull was still intact. Joe emptied it of water and pulled it above the tide line. He turned and saw the projecting land in the distance. Once, it had been Snak-a-pins, place of origin of the powerful Turtle clan. Now, it was a signpost, pointing the way home for the last member of that clan.

At some past time, a stroke of chance had pushed a large tree along on high storm waves. It had dropped the tree across the highest point of stone, and there it rested until that day. Joe saw the weathered, dry wood, and smiled until tears traced their way down his leathery cheeks.

The fire was warm and cheering. He collected a few clams and oysters from the rockweed-covered shore, and soon the pair of survivors were eating heartily. The darkness was absolute, unrelieved by the smallest glimmer of moon or stars. Only Joe's tiny fire broke the gloom, like a beacon of hope. It would be a cold night, but he knew Kane would warm him. When day came, he could go to the old home easily. The imminence of death became only a memory of something whose threat had not been fulfilled.

Joe sat up late that night, staring into the embers. He made his thanks to the Great Spirit for saving him. He recalled a story about these very islands. It was in earliest times, when Indians first came to Wanaqua, his old home. They discovered that a mighty battle was being fought here. Tchi-Manitou and Manetto, Good and Evil, were locked in deadly combat. The winner would rule over the people of this country. Since Manetto was very bad and responsible for such misfortune as death and famine, the Indians sided with the good spirit. For that he loved them, but the evil one was very powerful. The struggle went on for many generations, and the Indians often suffered great hardship on account of it. But one day, the evil one was seriously wounded. He broke off the fight and retreated into the thick woods of Wanaqua to lick his wounds. It was by sheer chance that a hunting party of Algonquin braves cornered him in a small cave. They managed to tie him up with cords of rawhide and were taking him to the good spirit, when Manetto used one great burst of his awesome strength and broke the ropes. Badly wounded, and very weak, he chose to flee rather than stand and fight. Taking the shortest route out of that territory, he ran across the Sound and to Long Island. A very mysterious thing, born of the black powers, happened. Every place where the evil foot touched water, a barren, rocky island formed to support it. These became known as the Steppingstone Islands (and are still called that to this day). Joe's island was one of these.

When Manetto reached the far shore, he was not satisfied with simple escape. He now wanted revenge against the spirit, and the Indians who had defeated him. He picked up every huge boulder in sight and hurled them back, toward Wanaqua.

Mute evidence of that titanic battle can be seen to this very day in many parts of the Bronx. There is the famous Rocking Stone, which sits perched where it fell in the present Bronx Zoo. It is said that the touch of a small child, on the right spot, is enough to set this boulder rocking. Yet a farmer with twenty oxen was once unable to tow it off its base of bedrock. Another proof is Split Rock, where Ann Hutchinson, an early settler, hid during Indian raids on her farm. Then there is Glover's Rock, where a handful of Continental militiamen under Colonel John Glover's command held off the vastly superior forces of General William

Howe's invasion long enough to allow George Washington to
prevent the destruction of his army, and the loss of the Revolu-
tionary War. There are other mementos of that ancient bom-
bardment. The Lion Rock, Saxon Stone, Tillie's Rock, all have
some part in Bronx history. But they played a part in the older
history of an earlier civilization, too.

So it was that Two Trees was saved by the footprint of a
devil. He sat and pondered that odd circumstance until he felt
the cold touch of snow against his face. Joe drew closer to the
warming fire and prepared to spend the dark time. Kane crept
against his side to make her warmth one with his. The cold was
to allow very little comfort during the coming hours, but morning would find them still survivors.

More than once, he thought longingly of the lost bearskin.
But it was gone now, having become just another part of his
past. He had had it, and now it was simply his no more. It was
like many vanished things. There were his parents, Tony,
Sheila, and now the robe.

As was quite typical of my friend Two Trees, he probably res-
urrected some old Indian saying that night. I imagine it would
have translated very roughly into something about "spilt milk."
That was the way he would have liked me to think he really felt
about his past life. I always let him feel that I did, but I knew
better. The Joe I knew was a sensitive man. He was a man who
had lived so much in his early years and so little in his later life.
The violence, romance, and danger of his past were in tremen-
dous contrast to the self-imposed exile at Hunter Island when I
knew him.

It often happened that I would find my eyes riveted to his face
when he told me about some obscure happening of his long ago.
He seldom looked at me when he told those tales. His gaze would
invariably find the deepest part of the campfire and fix there, as
if it was registering incalculably more than flames and ashes. At
those tellings, some strange metamorphosis born of his agitation
and enthusiasm would, with the help of my boyish imagination,
make him into a young brave again. As the flame light danced
and flickered, I could often see the years melt from Two Trees
until no gray colored his long hair, no wrinkle grooved his

leather cheeks. Sometimes when he told me of the past, and especially of Sheila, I noticed great tears well up to reflect the flame images. These, he surreptitiously brushed aside, not aware that I had seen. Perhaps those visions of him were only caused by some errant effect of the light or some other odd manifestation of physical law, but I like to think I sometimes saw the Joe of long ago, reliving the happy parts of his poor life. Yes, Joe would have liked me to think him a stoic, putting the past behind and never grieving for its loss, but it simply was not so.

20

To the Land of His Ancestors

When daylight was sufficient, Two Trees wasted no time in setting off. He followed the chain of rock islands, going from one stepping stone to the next. When he reached Hart Island, Joe stopped paddling for a short while. It was here that Eagle Feather used to take him to catch crabs when he was a little boy. He remembered the delectable taste of those crabs when Small Doe cooked them for the evening meal. He paddled on, faster now, perhaps compelled by some unconscious thought that all the years had never really happened after all. Two Trees was coming home.

He was on familiar ground once more. I don't know his names for the many islands, but I can almost feel his happiness as I visualize the route. Past the southeast end of Hart Island, he aimed for the little group of rocks now known as No Nation's Reef. Then on, and through one of the channels leading to the sluiceway that separates Hunter and Hog Islands. The looming bulk of Saxon Stone evoked memories of fishing days spent with the father of his boyhood. The canoe moved onto the silent waters of protected Vagabond Bay. Slowly, slowly, Two Trees paddled along the weeded shore, until he reached a tiny outcrop cloaked in groves of cedar. Here, he turned the bow toward a hidden lagoon and paddled into the tall bulrushes. He hid the boat among the thick rushes, and walked to the main island. Here, Two Trees and Kane drank from the sparkling spring that started somewhere in the rocky depths of

Hunter Island. The water was still as sweet and thirst-quenching as it had been years before.

With their thirst well satisfied, the two set off toward the old, hidden camp that had been home to one of them. The fallen leaves of winter carpeted the forest floor, softening it to their feet. Joe noticed that the familiarity his feet had grown to feel at the slightest touch of any road was somehow different here. It no longer held the urgent insistence of the many years passed. On these paths his feet felt satisfied, as if they had been walking over the other miles to seek out this very island. He smiled at the possibility that all the years of wanderlust had only been some subtle voice, gently calling him back here to the place of his beginning.

As they approached, he could see that the dense barricade of vines and brush was still intact. Many generations of Indian skill had made it what it was, undetectable and impenetrable. A few years of abandonment were not enough to undo all that. It wasn't yet time to enter the old home, though. First, he would kneel at the twin graves and speak long to Small Doe and Eagle Feather. It was right that they should know Two Trees, the son, had finally come home.

He found the unmarked graves with an ease only one who dug them could possess. Time had covered them with the Maker's grass and shrubbery. This pleased the Indian. He spent a long time in silent communion with the spirits of those who gave him life. He tried to explain the empty place in his heart, which still grieved for them both, and in a larger sense, for his lost race. He told them of his travels, and the many wonders he had seen. He told of his moments of pride, and also those of shame. He explained that he had not, for many reasons, been able to make a place in the white man's world. Joe ended by telling them he was still Indian, as they had made him, and so he would live and some day die, here in the old places. Having told these things, he felt somehow better than before. In the saying and thinking of all this, his plan had been finalized.

During all this time, Kane had sat silently by his side, in some primitive way knowing this was an important ritual that must not be interrupted. He spoke gently to her now, and she rose to follow. He entered the compound through the hidden portico, which had apparently been unused for almost eight years. Things were overgrown with weeds and creepers, but they were essentially as he had left them. The shelter was somewhat dilapidated, but that would be easily repaired. Even the stores of firewood were still stacked, ready for use. The foodstuffs he had stored away for that winter that he never spent here had not gone to waste. Two Trees could see the unmistakable signs of many little visitors. Squirrels, rabbits, mice, skunks, foxes, all had eaten their share. But the wax-sealed pots, with heavy rocks on top, had not been opened. The Indian pulled the seals from some of these and peered inside. Enough seed had survived to assure a planting in the spring. Yes, he would know the taste of fresh corn, beans, squash, and other foods once again.

That winter was not an easy one, but it was not as hard as some he had known. Joe cleared and cleaned the camp. He made it as comfortable as possible. The shoreline gave him many large clams, mussels, and oysters. The woods gave rabbits and squirrels for meat and fur. The snows came and went, and spring followed them. He planted and tended the garden, and by the next fall, had vegetables again. The rich waters provided many fish for smoking. Within a few seasons he had established anew the patterns of his youth.

Occasionally, he would see white men along the shores. He became adept at the Indian camouflage tricks of old. I can testify that Joe could stand in a shadow and become one with it. More than once I watched him seem to dematerialize before my eyes, only to laugh and appear behind me. He became expert at this hiding, and all that went with it to avoid any more contact with the whites who had hurt him so badly. A few times over the years he was forced to flee to the mainland woods as his father had. Now and then during that period, whites came. But they always went away again, and then Two Trees with his dog returned, for this was their home.

As the years went by, the hair along Kane's muzzle started to grow gray. Joe's mind knew that she was now a very old dog, but his heart was not prepared to accept that fact. During all her life, Kane's love for him had never faltered, but toward the end, her body could no longer keep up with him. She wanted to go on the hunting trail with her master, but she needed to rest frequently now. An opaque film grew gradually across the brilliant eyes of her youth, and vision began to fail. The day came when she could not rise from her fireside spot to join him on the chase. Joe understood. He made her as comfortable as possible, and went alone to gather food for them. He brought rabbits, but she seemed unable to chew them. He examined her teeth and saw that many were loose or gone completely. The Indian cut her food in small pieces and handfed her. She licked him weakly in thanks. By careful feeding and nursing, Joe kept the blind Kane with him for another year. By then, what remained was a shadow of the once-mighty giant she had been. The animal's pain was evident, and that night Joe prayed to Tchi-Manitou that she suffer no more. When he woke, the stillness of her body told him that she padded along happy trails now, in a place where he hoped to one day join her.

He took her poor body in his arms, and thought back over the many years since a pair of yellow eyes had warned him away from the pups. How wonderful it was that this one pup had come to have those same eyes, and had grown to love him for all the years since. For a moment he thought of walking to the city once more, to find another dog. But even as he thought it, the idea was rejected. Among all the millions of dogs in the world, no other would ever be Kane. Two Trees buried his friend that morning in the row with his mother and father. He was sure they would care for her well in the afterworld as they awaited his arrival.

There was a long period of silence. Only the few sounds of a winter night broke an utter quiet. I squeezed my eyes shut, trying to force this day's story into my brain. Please, please, I recall thinking, let me remember this for always. I had been allowed, by some quirk of time, to relive, with Two Trees, an epic adventure. He had told it in a classic fashion, giving great attention to the details that had made it live. All that remained now was for me not to forget it over the years ahead. Could I? I remember praying, as only a youngster can, that I be given a special strength to freeze each detail in my mind for always. I hoped that years to come would not tarnish this gleaming gift that had been given to a young white boy for safekeeping.

The silence had gone on for such a long time! I nervously asked if there was more to the story. "No," was the reply. He spoke again, though, and told me that after the burial of Kane, years had come and passed, one season leading into the next, and then he said, "But wait, there is more." He related how he had lived in peace and quiet on his island for many years. Here he touched his hair as if its silver would underline the years that had passed.

"Then" said Joe, "a strange thing happened here." He went on to describe how his peace and solitude were broken. He noticed that someone came often to these woods, and spent long periods of time watching the workings of the Maker. That person had been only a small nuisance at the start, but later he had begun to examine Joe's rabbit traps. Since that scared off the game, the Indian had been forced to reveal himself to this white child. His original intention had been to prevail upon the child to leave the traps alone. Instead, he had decided to talk to the boy for a while.

Then my friend took on a very formal attitude. He thanked me graciously for my patience in listening to the story of an old man. He said he knew I would forget some parts, but to tell it to my children some day, anyhow. I mustered all my abilities to look and sound offended that he could think I would forget. He only smiled and replied, "Tell it as well as you can. I will try to help you then, as well as I can."

He told me to go home. He knew it was late and that my parents would be worried. "Here, you have done all that you could, and all that I could have asked of you. Now the time has come for you to return to your own world. My fate, those things to be, will happen here. Go now, with my respect."

He had survived many perils during his long life. There had been cold, hunger, wild beasts, and even that unpredictable menace, man. But now, I could plainly see, he would soon succumb to a greater adversary than any of those. Time was the final factor for Two Trees. That hourglass, which held the sands of his existence, had run low. The last grains would shortly fall. It was obvious in the deep cough and glassy eyes of an ancient Indian. Now, thought I, is my time to act.

I did as he asked, and left. I made only a short goodbye, for I knew I would soon return. I didn't linger along the way as

usual, reliving incidents that had happened here and there. This
time I ran, a mission in my heart, along the paths and ways. I
knew my father would understand the plight of a dying man
and come with me to carry Joe to salvation. I knew that together we could bring him to my home. There, we would help
and nurse him, and he would live on. As with Indian summer,
Great Spirit would stay the progress of His seasons for the last
of a once-mighty Algonquin clan. He would do this. I knew it.

It was cold and cheerless, even though it was December 24. I
ran through the fields and shortcuts that would take me to my
house. It was Christmas Eve, but I hadn't really thought about
that all day. I remember it very clearly, and I want to empha-
size that there can be no doubt about the fact that it was indeed
the night before Christmas. As I passed the houses along my
way, I saw families in windows, framed like pictures, trimming
trees and wrapping gifts. There was the sound of joy from
happy homes. I ran past a group who sang, door to door, of
silence and peace. The Prince of Peace was to be born! Surely
that was a wonderful sign. I decided that He would certainly
help Joe's Great Spirit. I remember thinking, as I rounded the
corner toward my house on Stadium Avenue, that perhaps I
had missed an idea here. Maybe the two spirits were really one,
in the last evaluation.

I came up the block and saw the twin white birch trees that
grew in front of my house. Their white stood chalky against the
ink of not-so-early evening. As I drew closer, I saw a figure
near the front. It was my father. He noticed me, still at a good
distance, and I saw him stoop to put something down. Then he
started toward me. We met at the driveway. He started to speak
but my pent-up story cut him short. He told me to slow down
and help him with what he had been doing. I went to the steps
and saw that he had been about to hang our homemade wreath
on the door. As we finished, he listened quietly to my request
for help. He then said we would go inside and talk to my
mother.

When we got in the kitchen, my mother was ready to scold
me for my lateness, but Dad waved her to silence, and told her
the basics of my story. She agreed that we might put a cot in
the cellar, by the furnace. She also felt it was our duty to do
what we could. The decision was made. My father and I made

up a rough stretcher, and my mother gathered spare blankets for the cot. At dawn my father would come to help me carry Joe to our home.

No youngster sleeps very well on the night before Christmas, but that night in 1924 was even more special. Other kids were listening secretly for sounds of Santa, but I wanted only the light of day. When the first gray tendrils of dawn had crept low in the eastern sky, I was already dressed and ready. My father had apparently heard me, because he was prepared soon after. We took the stretcher and walked out the front door. Snow had fallen during the night and drifts reached up the steps. It wasn't too deep though, and it had stopped already, so it didn't hamper our speed very much. As we neared the island, I watched for animal tracks along our path. I pointed these out to my father, and identified the various species for him. He seemed pleased that I knew these things, or maybe, in retrospect, he was pleased at my pleasure in knowing. I showed him the trees and told him stories of ancient occurrences at various spots as we passed. The mood was a happy one. We would be near the Indian's camp soon, and we would accomplish our purpose.

We reached the camp enclosure, and I could see by the undisturbed snow that Joe had not been outside yet. I showed my father the hidden entrance, and we went through. Something was wrong. The dead ashes of last night's fire were drifted over by snow, and no smoke rose from the hole in the shelter's roof. It was much too cold for Joe to be without fire! I ran to the shelter flap and looked inside. Joe wasn't there!

Where could he be? There were no tracks in or outside the compound. That must mean he had gone out during the night before the snow started. If he had left while the snow was falling, I was sure I would have been able to spot the snowed-in depressions that his footprints would have left. I was nervous. He was in no way physically able to do much walking. What if the storm had caught him away from the camp and he had fallen? Even now, he might be out there in the thick woods dying of the cold. My father and I decided to separate and search the large island in opposite directions. I walked and called out all morning, and toward noon met my father again. He had seen nothing more than I had. We continued to search throughout the day, and when it was too dark to go on, my father made me come home. I knew he was right. What more could I do? But still, I felt I was deserting my friend.

Early next morning I was back on Hunter Island. I searched again, until I finally knew I would not find Joe. I went back to his camp and examined everything there for some possible clue. I could find nothing missing, and no sign that Joe had taken any of his meager belongings. I kindled a small fire and made the familiar Indian tea for myself. Then I sat before that same fireplace we had shared so many times and thought. His words, spoken the last time we sat here, came to mind. "My fate, those things to be, will happen here." That was his message for me, but I had not understood. I drank my tea and straightened things out so the place was as I had found it. Then I started slowly home. When I passed the thick pine grove at the crest of the island, I stopped and stood quietly in the heavy shadows. I recalled that Joe had sometimes gone here to listen for his father's voice in the sighing sounds of the wind. I listened silently for a very long time, and I never was sure if the wind voice told me or not, but I knew I would never see Joe Two Trees again.

The sky was clear as I walked toward my family's home. Stars appeared very quickly when the winter sun faded from the sky. As it darkened further, I saw the broad path of light called the Milky Way. A new glow lit it, the campfire of an Algonquin brave on his way home. Somewhere, a wigwam waited in a land of easy hunting, next to a similar shelter where a mother and father sat. I was very sure, however, that the wigwam was not quite vacant. In its entranceway, I could easily visualize two shining, yellow eyes, as they peered out hopefully, looking for the master.

Afterthoughts

John Milton, the blind poet, said that a book is the blood of an idea, preserved and embalmed, to be handed up from age to age, throughout all time. I hope you have found this to be such a book. What is it that after all these pages is still missing? Everyone loves a story that has a happy ending. I haven't given you that in the story of Joe Two Trees. The picture of a human being voluntarily divorcing himself from all others, and existing as a misanthrope for nearly sixty years, is quite another ending. But is this the story's end? I sincerely hope not, for then this book will have been written in vain. If you, the reader, will take time to tell this story to your children, perhaps it *will* have a happy ending. In his telling, Two Trees asked no more of my father than that he remember and retell these exploits. In that way, believed Joe, he would never be completely gone from the trails and trees of his beloved land. When you go to the quiet places that still remain within our steel and stone city, it is just possible that you could meet him. I know you won't see him as a person, but the vee of Canada geese obeying their ancient migratory imperative, or the furtive glance of a raccoon, the blaze of a gorgeous sunset, one of these, or all, will be Joe.

Don't lose him. When we allow the new to replace the old to such an extent, we will lose more than an ancient Indian story. Keep in mind that in our rush to meet the future, we must be sure to keep the past. Without its foundation, no structure stands for very long. As the Algonquin fell and was replaced in such a short time, so can we expect to fall unless we read a small lesson in the life that has passed.

Index

Adze, stone, 143–144
Alcohol, 131, 135–136, 138, 159–160
Algonquin Indians, xix–xx, 190
  Iroquois and, xxiii–xxiv
  Manhattan evacuated by, xxiv
  spelling of name of, xv
  See also Turtle Clan
Algonquin language, Two Trees's loss of, 141–142
American Museum of Natural History, 7, 22, 31
American Revolution, *see* Revolutionary War
Aquehonga (Bronx River), 39–40
Archaeology, philosophy of, xxi–xxii

Arrowheads
  Iroquois, xxiii–xxiv, 27–28
  making of, 23–24, 25, 27–28
  Two Trees's pouch of, 22–24, 33–34
Arthur Kill, 63
Axe, stone, 143–145

Bass, 170–172
Bears, 15–16, 43, 81–86, 112
Beginning, The, story of, 34
Blizzard, 67–74
"Bowman's Brook"-type incising, 13
Breakfast, Indian, 17
Bronck, Jonas, 40
Bronx, The, xix–xx
  official historian of, x, xx

Bronx, The *(cont.)*
  Pell's purchase of parts
    of, 42–43
Bronx Park, x
Bronx River (Aquehonga),
    39–40
Bronx Zoo, 178
Burial, Indian, xxii–xxiii

Canoe, Two Trees's, 141–
    154, 166, 168–177
Cass (former slave), 93–
    100, 102
Cave, Two Trees's winter
    in, 81–86
Civil War, 99, 133–136
Clay pot, making of, 7–19
Coal mine, Two Trees as
    laborer in, 89–100

Deadfalls, 67
Deer, 24, 43, 104, 114–119
Delaware Indians, 58
Dog, Two Trees's, 123–184
    naming of, 142
  Two Trees saved by,
    160–164
Dried food (pimekan), 17
Ducks, hunting of, 25, 63–
    65
Dugout canoe, Two Trees's,
    141–154, 166, 168–177

Eagle Feather (Two Trees's

father), 23, 45–46, 58,
    111, 142
  boat hidden by, 154
  death of, 46–47
  grave of, 182
  honey, escapade of, 151–
    152
  knife made by, 52
  training of Two Trees by,
    72, 76, 175
Eagles, 171
Earth Mother, 34
Elm tree bark, 10

Farming
  Indian method of, 6–7,
    11, 183
  for Sheila, 129–130
Fire-making, 65
Fire pits, archaeological
    excavation of, xxi–xxiii
Fishing, 39–40, 170–171
  by net, 30–33
  through the ice, 66, 75–
    76
Flaking, 27, 144
Frostbite, 73

Glen Island, xxv
Glover, John, 178–179
Glover's Rock, 24, 178–179
Good and Evil, 34
Gray squirrel, 68, 74–75
Great Spirit (Tchi-Manitou;

Great Spirit *(cont.)*
Maker-of-All), xxiii, 5,
28–29, 65, 74, 101, 129
bears given by, 84–85
Indian Summer and, 25–
26, 84
Manetto's struggle with,
178
"medicine" of, *see*
"Medicine"
projects inspired by, 8

Happy Hunting Ground,
xxii, 188
Hart Island, xxv, 181
Hell Gate (Monatun), 40,
168, 170, 172–177
Herbs, 9, 14–15, 19–20
Hiawatha, 43
High Island, xxv
Hog Island, 181
Howe, Sir William, 45*n*,
178–179
Hudson River, 102–110,
118–120, 134
Two Trees's trips on,
146–154, 168–170
Hunter Island, ix, xxv, 3
bluish-gray clay of, 10
Two Trees's home on, 6–
7, 182–183
Two Trees's return to,
151, 167–183
Hutchinson, Ann, 178

Indian Summer, 25–26, 81,
84, 126, 167
Insect control in farming,
6–7
Iroquois Indians, xxiii–xxiv,
27–28, 43, 101

Joe, *see* Two Trees, Joe

Kane (dog), 123–184
naming of, 142
Two Trees saved by,
160–164
Kazimiroff, Theodore L.,
Sr., ix–xi, xix–xxv
as dentist, ix–x, xx
historical and
archaeological
collection of, xx
parents of, 12, 34, 186–
187
See also Two Trees, Joe
—author's father and
Keskeskek, xx
Kingsbridge Historical
Society, x

Lady bugs, 7
Lenni Lenape, 58
Lion Rock, 4, 179
Long Canoe (Two Trees's
great-grandfather), 44,
45
Long Island Sound, xxv,
172–173

Manetto, 10, 164, 178
Maker-of-All, *see* Great
    Spirit
Manhattan
    Algonquins in, xxiv
    bear and deer of, 43
    Two Trees in, *see* New
        York City
Marriage, Indian, 39
"Medicine," 9–10, 19–20,
    167
    pottery marks, 13
Medicine men, 20
Mellert, Miss, 34
Milky Way, xxiii, 188
Milton, John, 189
Mishow, 40, 41, 72
Monatun (Hell Gate), 40,
    168, 170, 172–177
Morning Flower (Two
    Trees's grandmother),
    45
Mushoon, *see* Dugout
    canoe

Net fishing, 30–33
New Jersey, Two Trees in,
    63–80
    Two Trees survives
        blizzard, 67–74
New York Botanical
    Garden, x, xxv
New York City, Two Trees
    in, 49–56, 155–164
    Two Trees gets drunk
        and is almost killed,
        159–162
    Two Trees kills a robber,
        54–56
New York State, upper,
    Two Trees in, 101–154
New York Zoological
    Society, x
No Nation's Reef, 181

Orchard Beach, 3, 40
Outerbridge Crossing, 63
Oyster-shell powder, 10–11

Pelham Bay Park
    author's father and, ix–
        xi, xxv
    Pell's purchase of, 42–43
    Saxon Stone in, 30, 179
    See also Hunter Island;
        Orchard Beach; Twin
        Island
Pell, Thomas, 42–43
Pennsylvania, 65, 66, 78
    Two Trees in, 80–101
        coal mining, 89–100
Pimekan, 17
Pottery, making of, 7–19
Praying mantises, 7
Pressure flaking, 27

Rabbits
    snares for, 4, 67, 68, 114,
        185

Rabbits *(cont.)*
  Two Trees's pet, 74, 76–79
Red Dawn (Two Trees's grandfather), 45
Revolutionary War, 45, 178–179
Riverdale, xxv
  fire pit in, xxi–xxiii
Rocking Stone, 178

Sachem, 41
Sassafras, 14
Saxon Stone, 30, 179
"Scrapers," 27, 144
Sewan (wampum), xxiv
Sewan-Hacky, 39–40
Sheila (Two Trees's lover), 105–139, 145, 147, 180
Shore Road, 42
Siwanoy Indians, 39, 43
Skins, preparing, 84
Sky Woman, 34
Slaves, escaped, 80, 93–100
Small Doe (Two Trees's mother), 23, 45, 152, 181, 182
  death of, 47
Smallpox (spotted sickness), 44
Snak-a-pins, 39–40, 168, 177
Snow, 64, 66, 68–77, 85
Snowshoes, 73
Snowy owl, 68, 72, 75

"Soap," wet sand as, 32, 119
Solecki, Ralph S., "Foreword" by, ix–xi
Split Rock, 178
Squirrel, gray, 68, 74–75
Staten Island, Two Trees on, 56–64
Stone tools, 24, 27, 143–145
Sumac tea, 9, 12, 14

Tchi-Manitou, *see* Great Spirit
Tea, 9, 12, 14
Thomas Pell Wildlife Sanctuary, x
Threes, significance of, 20
Tillie's Rock, 179
Tony (Two Trees's friend), 53–56, 58, 95–96, 102–103
  Two Trees's search for, 151, 153, 156–160
Tools, stone, 24, 27, 143–145
Torn Moccasin, 44
Trout, 66, 75–76
Turtle Clan, x, 47
  formation of, 39–42
  last council of, 43–44
Turtle Cove, 24–25, 45
Twin Island, 3, 4, 45–46
Two Trees, Joe
  author's father and, xix–

Two Trees, Joe *(cont.)*
    xx, xxv, 3–36, 101–
    102, 187–188
        meeting, 3–5, 185
    forefathers of, 45
    naming of, 45–46, 51
    passim

Underground Railway, 80*n*,
    94

Vagabond Bay, 23, 31, 46,
    181

Wampum, xxiv
Wanaqua, xx, 178
Washington, George, 179

Weckquaesgek tribe, xxv
Westchester County, xxiv,
    43
Whiskey, 131, 135–136, 138
White Americans,
    relationship of Indians
    to, 87–88, 90–91, 99,
    100, 138
Wigwams, 40–41, 67–78
Winter, 15, 21, 47–48, 85,
    103–104, 127–129, 183
    of blizzard, 64–77
    Indian Summer as
    preparation for, 25–26,
    84
Woman, Two Trees's, *see*
    Sheila

LAUREL

The Laurel logo stands for the finest in contemporary fiction and nonfiction

A NEW GUERNSEY-HUMPHRY MILKEY
by Richard Llewellyn

I HEARD THE OWL CALL MY NAME
by Margaret Craven

THE HUMAN FACTOR
by Wayne Sawyer

DELIVERANCE
by James Dickey

W BEACH STREET QUARTET TALE
by James Baldwin

GREAT JEWISH SHORT STORIES
by Saul Bellow, Editor

GREAT RUSSIAN SHORT STORIES
by Norris Houghton, Editor

GREAT SOVIET SHORT STORIES
by F.D. Reeve, Editor

by James Stephen

At your local bookstore or use this handy page for ordering:

DELL READERS SERVICE, DEPT. DLT
P.O. Box 5057, Des Plaines, IL. 60017-5057

Please send me the above title(s). I am enclosing $_____
and $2.00 per order to cover shipping and handling. Send check or
money order—no cash or C.O.D.s please.

DATE DUE

DISCARD

Ms.

Address

City/State

GRIERSON LIB SPAULDING JR HIGH

T 19038

DLT-8/91

Prices and availability
for delivery.